Contents

Introduction

While tracing the origin, development and demise of Belfast folk songs in my first book, *Belfast, City of Song*, I was continually unearthing children's street games and decided that they deserved to be published in a book of their own. The material in this book has been culled from many sources and I have brought together a comprehensive range of children's games played throughout Ireland, complete with music notation, game instructions and background notes setting each game in its historical perspective. Furthermore, I have recorded a cassette tape – also called *Boys and Girls, Come Out To Play* – of the songs that accompany the games to complement the publication.

In this collection I have included long forgotten games, such as "Thread the Needle" and "Here Is One Knight" – games of great antiquity that give us glimpses of the Middle Ages. There are also the more popular games, such as "Nuts in May", "The Farmer's in His Den" and "Briar Rosebud" that are as familiar to the children of Europe and America as they are to the children of Ireland. These are the games that have survived "the usually rubbing or blurring consequent on long use among unlettered people". The versions I have given are not the definitive ones and, inevitably, readers will have different ways of playing these games. This does not detract from them but emphasises the tenacity of children's folklore, the survival of which has defied time and place.

I had always thought that, particularly in Belfast, we had an indigenous repertoire of children's games, but that is not the case. Most of the games that exist in Belfast are to be found throughout Ireland and Great Britain – a cultural network of children's games largely unaffected by regional differences.

One of the remarkable things about these games is that they are all generally played using only three formations: a ring, an arch or a straight line. There are some exceptions, like the "Big Ship Sails", "Hurley Burley" and "Relievio". It is also quite amazing that such a confined area as the terraced street has spawned such a wide spectrum of children's games with their own street language and lore.

Some of these games have an underlying moral code and give the children an introduction to rites of passage, details of which are contained in the songs about birth, love, courtship, marriage, sickness and death. Family structures are depicted with mammies and grannies featuring regularly, though daddies and grandpas are largely ignored. Widows or single girls are considered to be at odds with the family unit and while widows are lampooned, the single girls are encouraged to "get a man". Oddly enough, God is never mentioned in any of these games. This is hardly surprising, since many of the May-time games, for example, are associated with pagan rituals, such as dancing around the May tree or, its substitute, the Maypole. This was known as tree worship. "Sally Walker/Water" is a game frequently associated with well worship, which was widely practised throughout Ireland. Nowadays, some people bring home water from holy wells, because they believe that it has special healing powers.

The games have an educational value, teaching children to count and to recite the alphabet or the months of the year, and many games mention flowers or plants. The lyrics are peppered with the rhymes and rhythms of poetry, while the melodies are instantly appealing. The children learn to sing, dance and co-ordinate their body movements and can act out tragic dramas like "Briar Rosebud" or "Jenny Jo". Skipping, ball and clapping games can develop a good memory, dexterity and co-ordination due to the complex and repetitive actions of the games. There is even room to develop leadership qualities for those who want to organise, but they will also soon learn that they will have to take their place in the queue along with everybody else.

Over a century ago W. H. Patterson was concerned that many games were falling out of favour with the children and he wrote that "the children of the well-to-do ... might find pleasure for themselves ... by learning such games". A few years later, under the guiding influence of the eminent folk-song collector Cecil Sharp, a movement started in England dedicated to instilling old values in the minds of children blighted by the effects of the Industrial Revolution. A programme of reform was drawn up to educate children in clubs, play centres and schools using traditional street games.

Almost a century later we are fighting a similar crusade with the same philosophy of instilling old values into young hearts and minds by using children's street games to achieve these objectives. We are confronted with the same problem of a valuable tradition in decline, but for different reasons. The "street play-ground" is overrun with motor-cars, which make the streets dangerous to play in, and the boisterous nature of some of the games is often a nuisance to some neighbourhoods. Our technological age has brought sedentary leisure and pleasure at the press of a button. Television, video, computer games and hi-fis have taken children off the streets in droves. They do not need these games any more for their stimulation and entertainment.

As a result, educationalists are now attempting to reintroduce these street games into the school curriculum. Furthermore, in the divided society of the North of Ireland, traditional street games are being used to promote the idea of a common cultural heritage to bridge the gap between the two communities.

It is my hope that this book and tape will complement the valuable work being carried out in these areas and help to bring these games back on the streets where they belong. One of the objectives of my first book, *Belfast, City of Song*, was to create an awareness of the wealth and variety of long-forgotten Belfast folk songs. Three years later groups such as Patrick Street and Craobh Rua and singers such as Ben Sands and Gemma Hasson are recording songs from that book, and other singers are including them in their live performances, and I am continually being asked to perform these songs for audiences other than folk-music enthusiasts. I hope that this book will have even greater success.

1: Once I Courted

Here stands a lady on a mountain,
Who she is I do not know.
All she wants is gold and silver,
All she wants is a nice young man.

Here Is One Knight

This is sometimes known as "There Were Three Dukes/Brethren out of Spain", or in the case of Dublin with its broad nasal accent: "There Were Three Jews". It is a game that recalls the days when European merchants sent their ambassadors to foreign countries or came themselves in person to choose a wife. Occasionally, children dress up in old costumes, complete with headgear to get into the continental spirit of the game. The words are a well-scripted drama loaded with sarcasm, barbs and insults, with references to "saucy knight" and "scour your spurs". The inference is that only rich people can afford to wear gleaming spurs and that anybody who comes courting with dirty spurs is unseemly and beneath contempt. The knight replies caustically that his spurs were bought in some far-off exotic place and not in these backwoods! The game is generally followed by "Pray, Pretty Miss!"

"Here Is One Knight" was first collected in 1765 and variations are known throughout the Continent, Scandinavia, North America, Chile and Brazil.

Here is one knight has come from Spain
A courting of your daughter Jane.

My daughter Jane she is too young
And can't abide your flattering tongue.

Go home, go home, you saucy knight
And scour your spurs till they grow bright.

My spurs, my spurs, they owe you naught
For in your land they were not bought.

Then fare you well, my lady gay
I'll come and court some other day.

Come back, come back, you Spanish knight
And choose the one you love so bright.

The fairest one that I do see
Is bonnie Jane, so come to me.

All the children stand in a straight line and one is chosen as mother. A knight is picked to advance and retire in front of the line. All the children sing the first verse. The mother sings the second and third verses. The knight sings the fourth and fifth verses. The children sing the sixth verse and the knight sings the last verse.

In some versions of the song the last line becomes a question: "Is bonnie Jane, will you come to me?" The game continues as "Pray, Pretty Miss" sung to the tune of "Nuts in May".

Lady on the Mountain

Occasionally known as "Yonder Stands a Lady" or "The Keys of Heaven", this game is now almost forgotten, except for the first four lines which are used as a skipping rhyme. The phrase "coach and chair" is a mispronunciation of "cosy chair", which is the same as a version collected in 1846. It also refers to "a nice armchair" or "a nice easy chair to sit in and comb your yellow hair" – a good example of how the oral tradition can preserve words, even though their original meaning has long since been forgotten.

There stands a lady on the mountain,
Who she is I cannot tell.
All she wants is gold and silver,
All she wants is a nice young man.
Madam, will you walk it?
Madam, will you talk it?
Madam, will you marry me?

No!

Not if I buy you the keys of Heaven?
Not if I buy you a coach and chair?
Not if I buy you a comb of silver
To place in your bonny, bonny hair?

No!

All the children form a circle and hold hands. One child stands in the centre. The rest walk around her and sing the first verse. The child in the middle gives a very indignant "No!" to all the questions and the singing continues with verse two.

Poor Mary Sits A-Weeping

Sean O'Casey had a version of this game in his autobiography *I Knock at the Door*. It was widely played throughout Great Britain and Ireland at the end of the last century. The earliest collected version dates back to 1880. Many of the versions do not make it very clear what Mary is weeping for, though in Scotland she weeps for her "true lover dead". In this version she is weeping for "the want of a man" and is, therefore, entitled to "stand up and choose" her lover. The game begins mournfully like a funeral game but ends happily with Mary choosing a lover. It is also played in Australia and New Zealand.

Poor Mary sits a-weeping, a-weeping, a-weeping,
Poor Mary sits a-weeping, on a bright summer day.

Pray, tell us what you're weeping for, a-weeping for, a-weeping for,
Pray, tell us what you're weeping for, on a bright summer day.

I'm weeping for my true love, my true love, my true love,
I'm weeping for my true love, on a bright summer day.

Stand up and choose your lover, your lover, your lover,
Stand up and choose your lover, on a bright summer day.

The children form a ring and hold hands, while "Mary" kneels in the middle of the circle and covers her face with her hands. The circle of children dance around her and sing the first and second verses. Mary uncovers her face to answer the question and sings verse three. The circle of children sing the last verse, during which Mary stands up and looks around to choose her lover, who goes to the centre of the circle. Mary joins the circle and the game begins again with the chosen lover in the centre.

Pray, Pretty Miss

This is such a short game that it generally gets tagged onto other games, notably "Here Is One Knight". It is a very straightforward singing game with the addition of a colourful and colloquial verse three. It is sung to the tune of "Nuts in May".

Pray, pretty Miss, will you come out,
Will you come out, will you come out?
Pray, pretty Miss, will you come out
To help us on with our dancing?

No!

The proud wee girl, she won't come out,
She won't come out, she won't come out.
The proud wee girl, she won't come out
To help us on with our dancing.

Or

You dirty wee scut, you wouldn't come out,
You wouldn't come out, you wouldn't
*   come out.*
You dirty wee scut, you wouldn't come out
To help us on with our dancing.

Pray, pretty Miss, will you come out,
Will you come out, will you come out?
Pray, pretty Miss, will you come out
To help us on with our dancing?

Yes!

Now we've got the pretty fair maid,
The pretty fair maid, the pretty fair maid.
Now we've got the pretty fair maid
To help us on with our dancing.

All the players form a line, except two, who stand facing the line. These two join hands crosswise and then advance and retire as they sing the first verse to the child at the end of the line. When the first child refuses to join them, they dance around and sing the second verse. They continue to sing the first verse, until they get the answer "yes". The child at the end of the line eventually says "yes", joins the other two and all three dance around and sing the third verse. The three children now advance and retire, singing the first verse as they go to another child at the end of the line. The game continues until they all say "yes".

Round about the Ladies

This game was extremely popular at the end of the last century when it was better known as "Round and Round the Village". It is very similar to "Dusty Bluebells", which eventually replaced it in popularity during this century.

In 1880 it was noted that after a marriage took place in the bride's house, the marriage party made a circuit around the village. This is a good example of how a children's game can evolve or adapt to new surroundings, when the significance of names or customs is long forgotten. The last verse is, of course, localised to wherever the song is sung, as long as it has two syllables, as in "Chase him back to Dublin".

Marching round the ladies, marching round the ladies
Marching round the ladies, as you have done before.

In and out the windows, in and out the windows
In and out the windows, as you have done before.

Stand and face your lover, stand and face your lover
Stand and face your lover, as you have done before.

Follow him (her) to London, follow him (her) to London
Follow him (her) to London, as you have done before.

Chase him (her) back to Belfast, chase him (her) back to Belfast
Chase him (her) back to Belfast, as you have done before.

All the children form a circle and hold hands. One child marches around the outside of the circle as the first verse is sung. During the second verse all the children in the circle raise their hands to form an arch and the child who is on the outside of the circle threads his/her way around the circle. During the third verse the child goes to the centre of the circle and stands in front of a chosen lover. During the fourth verse the child who was originally on the outside of the circle rushes away from the circle, quickly followed by the chosen lover. During the last verse they both return and the chase continues around the outside of the circle. The first child tries to get to the space left vacant by the chosen lover. If caught, he/she must retire from the game. In any case, the first player is replaced on the outside by the chosen lover. The game continues until everybody has had their turn on the outside of the circle.

Round about the Punchbowl

This game was not widely known during this century or the last, and only three versions were published by A. B. Gomme in 1894. One was from Scotland, one was from Belfast and this version is from County Louth. It is a marriage game, which explains its name. Punch was made by mixing several alcoholic beverages in a bowl and was normally drunk at celebrations such as weddings. No melody survives, but the song has the same metre as "Nuts in May".

Round about the punchbowl, one, two, three,
Open the gates and let the bride through.

Half-a-crown to know his name, to know his name,
*   to know his name,*
Half-a-crown to know his name,
On a cold and frosty morning.

Ah! (Michael Matthews) is his name, is his name,
*   is his name,*
(Michael Matthews) is his name,
On a cold and frosty morning.

Half-a-crown to know her name, to know her name,
*   to know her name,*
Half-a-crown to know her name,
On a cold and frosty morning.

(Annie Kennan) is her name, is her name, is her
*   name,*
(Annie Kennan) is her name,
On a cold and frosty morning.

They'll be married in the morning
Round about the punchbowl, HI!

The first and last verses are recited. The children form a ring and curtsey during the first verse as they say emphatically: "one, two, three"; the last one to raise her head is chosen as the bride. She is led out of the ring by another child, who asks her in confidence to whom she is engaged, and the two return to the circle through the raised arms, which form the gates. All the children then sing the second verse. The girl who has been told the name sings the next verse about Michael Matthews, who goes into the centre of the circle; all the other children sing the fourth verse. Annie Kennan joins her lover in the circle. The children walk around the couple and recite the last verse. "Hi" is "guldered" at the tops of their voices and the game continues until everybody is married!

Three Dukes

"Three Dukes" is another game peppered with the same sentiments as "Here Is One Knight": arrogance, scorn and insult. It is a similar drama about the arrival from another country of suitors with "black complexions" seeking the hand of a maiden. This is an engaging courtship game where each side tries to outdo the other with their sarcasm and scathing insults – but in the end they all live happily ever after with their newly found wives and husbands. The game was well known in the nineteenth century and was played throughout the Continent and North and South America.

Here come three dukes a-riding, a-riding, a-riding,
Here come three dukes a-riding, with a Tanzy, tir-ra-lee.

What are you riding here for, here for, here for,
What are you riding here for, with a Tanzy, tir-ra-lee?

We're riding here to marry, to marry, to marry,
We're riding here to marry, with a Tanzy, tir-ra-lee.

Then marry one of us, Sirs, us, Sirs, us, Sirs,
Then marry one of us, Sirs, with a Tanzy, tir-ra-lee.

You're all too young to marry, to marry, to marry,
You're all too young to marry, with a Tanzy, tir-ra-lee.

We're old enough for you, Sirs, you, Sirs, you, Sirs,
We're old enough for you, Sirs, with a Tanzy, tir-ra-lee.

You're all as stiff as pokers, pokers, pokers,
You're all as stiff as pokers, with a Tanzy, tir-ra-lee.

We're not as stiff as you, Sirs, you, Sirs, you, Sirs,
We're not as stiff as you, Sirs, with a Tanzy, tir-ra-lee.

You're all too black and dirty, dirty, dirty,
You're all too black and dirty, with a Tanzy, tir-ra-lee.

We're not as black as you, Sirs, you, Sirs, you, Sirs,
We're not as black as you, Sirs, with a Tanzy, tir-ra-lee.

Yet we can bow to you, Sirs, to you, Sirs, to you, Sirs,
Yet we can bow to you, Sirs, with a Tanzy, tir-ra-lee.

Through the kitchen, through the hall,
We choose the fairest of you all.
The fairest one that I can see
Is pretty Miss (Sarah), come here to me.

Three boys stand in a line facing the girls, who are holding hands. The boys advance towards the girls as they sing the first verse and imitate riding a horse. During the rest of the song the boys sing the uneven verses and recite verse twelve, while the girls sing the even verses and verse eleven. As the girls sing their verses they should display appropriate emotions; in verse four they behave shyly, in verse six they are indignant, in verse eight they become as stiff as pokers or touch their toes to prove they are not, and in verse eleven they bow humbly before their suitors. Similarly, in verses five, seven and nine the dukes are arrogant, sarcastic and contemptuous. At verse twelve, when the girl is named, she crosses over to join the dukes and holds hands with them. The game then continues as they sing: "Here come four dukes" – and ends when the maidens have all been named and have joined the dukes in their line.

2: When I Was Married

Now you are married, life enjoy,
First a girl and then a boy,
Seven years after and seven years to come,
Please, young couple, kiss and have done.

Here's an Oul' Widow

William Carleton, the great County Tyrone writer of the nineteenth century, describes a similar children's marriage game called "Silly Old Man" at Larry MacFarland's wake in his book *Traits and Legends of the Irish Peasantry*, first published in 1830. Other versions describe an "old soldier" returning from the war in search of a wife.

A County Louth version collected in the 1890s has "Three Dukes" grafted onto it with a refrain "dilcy, dulcy officer".

Another version from Newfoundland has the first line: "There was an old woman lived in Athlone".

Oh, here's an oul' widow, she lies alone,
She lies alone, she lies alone,
Oh, here's an oul' widow, she lies alone,
She wants a man and she can't get one.

Chorus:
Choose one, choose two,
Choose the fairest of you,
The fairest one that I can see,
Is (Paddy McGuffin), come over to me.

And now she's married and tied till a bag,
And tied till a bag, and tied till a bag,
And now she's married and tied till a bag,
And married a man with a wooden leg.

Chorus

All the children form a ring and join hands. A girl takes her place in the middle of the circle as the "oul' widow". The rest of the children walk around her and sing the first verse. Having chosen Paddy, he joins the "widow" in the centre of the circle. The children resume their walking around the "married couple" and sing the second verse; another husband is chosen after the second chorus is sung. In Belfast parlance a bag is an old hag.

Here's a Poor Widow from Sandy Row

This is an excellent example of a game that has been adopted into the local body of street games. The game is widely known as "Lady of the Land", which has become "Babyland", "Babylon", "Sandiland" and of course "Sandy Row". The game has echoes of the hiring fair with its reference to "please take one in" and "goodbye, Nellie, goodbye" as the family parts company. The Belfast version is the only one which refers to a "winder" (one of the trades in the linen industry), although Halliwell's 1849 version had the line: "one can sit in the arbour and spin". In localising the first two lines the original rhyme has been lost and should be: "Here comes an old woman from Sandiland with all her children by the hand".

Here's a poor widow from Sandy Row
With all her children behind her.
One can knit and one can sew
And one can make a winder go,
Please take one in, please take one in.

Now, poor (Nellie), she is gone
Without a farthing in her hand.
Nothing but a guinea gold ring
Goodbye, (Nellie), goodbye.
Goodbye, mother, goodbye.

Two of the bigger girls are chosen, one to represent the widow and one to represent the lady. The lady stands by herself, a little distance away from the widow, while the rest of the children arrange themselves on either side of the widow, with whom they advance and retire hand in hand while singing. At the last line of the first verse the lady chooses one of the children, who then stands or sits behind her. The widow and the children continue to sing the last verse. The game continues until all the children have been "taken" by the lady.

My Aunt Jane

Surely the national anthem of Belfast, this is another children's song which is peculiar to the north-east of Ireland. The song celebrates one of the dying institutions of terraced streets – the corner shop. Ironically, this song has become more popular with adults than it has with children, no doubt because of the significance the wee shop had in back-street life. It beautifully encapsulates a slower way of life that has now disappeared, with its tea in a tin, baps with sugar on top, conversation lozenges and the pride in the white stone step. Verses four and five are less well known and were collected by Richard Hayward.

My Aunt Jane, she took me in,
She gave me tea out of her wee tin,
Half a bap with sugar on the top,   } Repeat
Three black lumps out of her wee shop.

My Aunt Jane has a bell at the door,
A white stone step and a clean swept floor,
Candy apples and hard green pears,   } Repeat
Conversation lozenges.

My Aunt Jane, she's so smart,
She bakes wee rings in an apple tart,
And when Hallowe'en comes round,   } Repeat
Fornenst that tart I'm always found.

My Aunt Jane, she'll dance a jig,
And sing a ballad round a wee sweetie pig,
Wee red eyes and a cord for a tail,   } Repeat
Hanging in a bunch from a farthing nail.

My Aunt Jane has a great wee shop,
Lucky bags and lime juice rock,
Cinnamon lumps and yellow man, } Repeat
And big brandy balls in a bright tin can.

My Aunt Jane, she took me in,
She gave me tea out of her wee tin,
Half a bap with sugar on the top, } Repeat
Three black lumps out of her wee shop.

I have not come across any instructions for this as a street game, but I have decided to include it in the collection, since it is so widely known and sung. It is an example of one of the indigenous children's songs we have.

Pretty Little Girl of Mine

This is a marriage/courtship game which is very similar to "Sally Walker", especially in relation to its comments about morality. This game, however, involves more interesting detail, such as the bringing of a bottle of wine and a biscuit to celebrate the betrothal, and the kneeling down for the marriage ceremony. The inclusion of a biscuit is a modern addition to the vocabulary of the game, which was widely played at the end of the last century. It is sung to the tune of "Roman Soldiers".

See what a pretty little girl I am,
She gave me many a bottle of wine,
Many a bottle of wine and a biscuit too,
See what a pretty little girl can do.

Down on the carpet you shall kneel,
As the grass grows in your fiel',
Stand up straight upon your feet,
And choose the one you love so sweet.

Now you are married, life enjoy,
First a girl and then a boy,
Seven years after and seven years to come,
Please, young couple, kiss and have done.

All the children form a circle and join hands around one child, who stands in the centre. The circle moves around and sings. The child in the centre follows the instructions of the game as they are sung: kneeling down, or standing up to choose a partner who goes into the centre of the circle. The couple kiss during the last line. The first child who was in the centre now joins the circle, leaving her partner there; the game continues until all have had their turn in the centre.

Sally Walker

Sometimes known as "Sally Water", this is a simple marriage/courtship game that was extremely popular at the end of the last century. "Sally Walker" is very similar to "Pretty Little Girl of Mine", with almost identical last verses in both games. Note that the partner is chosen for love, while marriage is solely for the procreation of children.

Rise, Sally Walker, rise, Sally Ken,
Rise, Sally Walker, follow young men,
Choose to the East and choose to the West,
Choose to the very one you love best.

Marriage comfort and marriage joy,
First a girl and then a boy,
Seven years after, seven years to come,
Fire on the mountain, kiss and run.

All the children form a circle, join hands and begin singing as they move around one child, who has been chosen to kneel or sit in the centre of the circle. The chosen player in the centre covers his or her face with their hands and pretends to cry. When the children start to sing: "Rise, Sally Walker", the player in the middle stands up and chooses a child from the circle, who also goes to the centre.

The two in the centre dance around, while the rest of the children sing the second verse. They kiss when the word "kiss" is sung. When the word "run" is sung, the child who was first in the centre runs and joins the circle, leaving the other child in the centre. The game continues as before until everybody has had their turn in the centre of the circle.

The Farmer's in His Den

This is one of the best-known children's games today, yet it was not familiar at the end of the last century. It is a very good example of how some ring games can end in a climax of thumping or horseplay.

The last verse of a Dublin version is very graphic in detail: "The bone won't crack, the bone won't crack, E – I – E – I, the bone won't crack." The refrain is also known as "Heigh-ho, my deario" or "Heigh-ho, my daddio". "Denn" is an old English word meaning a clearing in a wood. In America the game is known as "The Farmer's in His Dell", which is a valley or small hollow with tree-clad sides. Wherever it is sung, it is still a good role model for marital bliss and domesticity.

The children form a ring and a boy stands in the middle, while the circle of players move around him and sing the first verse:

> *The farmer's in his den, the farmer's in his den,*
> *Heigh ho for rowley-o, the farmer's in his den.*
>
> *The farmer wants a wife, the farmer wants a wife,*
> *Heigh ho for rowley-o, the farmer wants a wife.*

The boy in the middle of the circle picks out a girl to be his wife and she joins him while the singing continues:

> *The wife wants a child, the wife wants a child,*
> *Heigh ho for rowley-o, the wife wants a child.*

The wife in the middle of the circle picks a little boy or a little girl, who joins the farmer and the wife in the circle; the singing continues:

> *The child wants a nurse, the child wants a nurse,*
> *Heigh ho for rowley-o, the child wants a nurse.*

The little boy or girl in the middle of the circle picks a young girl as a nurse, who joins the farmer, the wife and the child in the circle; the singing continues:

> *The nurse wants a dog, the nurse wants a dog,*
> *Heigh ho for rowley-o, the nurse wants a dog.*

The nurse usually selects a boy to join the farmer, the wife, the child and the nurse in the circle; the singing continues:

> *The dog wants a bone, the dog wants a bone,*
> *Heigh ho for rowley-o, the dog wants a bone.*

The "dog" usually picks another boy to join the farmer, the wife, the child, the nurse and the dog in the circle; the singing continues:

> *The bone is left alone, the bone is left alone,*
> *Heigh ho for rowley-o, the bone is left alone.*

At this stage everybody runs away and leaves the "bone" by himself. However, the "bone" can now become the farmer and the game starts all over again. In some versions the last verse is:

> *We all pat the bone, we all pat the bone,*
> *Heigh ho for rowley-o, we all pat the bone.*

While this is being sung all the children gather around the "bone" and pat or thump him on the head or the back.

Up the Heathery Mountain

I am intrigued by this marriage game because it is obviously derived from a poem of the same name written by the Donegal poet William Allingham. He in turn borrowed from a Scottish song called "Charlie Is My Darling", first published in 1821.

It is uncharacteristic for a children's game to be vulgar. This one uses such terms as "hugging and cuddling" to describe courting; Annie already has a baby and a lot of physical contact is required during the game. In effect, it does not set a good moral example for the children to follow; this may explain why the game did not survive well. Even by the end of the last century it was almost extinct. It is interesting to note that the baking of the bridal cake and the eating of it by the bride and groom were as important to the marriage ceremony then as they are now. In Great Britain the game was known as "All the Boys in Our Town" and was first collected in 1847.

Up the heathery mountain and down the rushy glen,
We daren't go a-hunting for Conor and his men,
We are all sally butchers but one game cock,
And that's lovely (Johnny), the flower of the flock.
He's the flower of the flock, he's the keeper of the glen,
He courted (Annie Nelson) before he was a man,
He hugged her, he cuddled her, he took her on his knee,
Saying, my dear (Annie), won't you marry me?

(Annie) made a pudding so nice and so sweet,
And (Johnny) got his knife and cut it round and neat,
Saying, taste love, taste love, don't say nay,
Perhaps tomorrow morning will be our wedding day.
With rings on our fingers and bells on our toes,
And a little baby in her arms and that's the way she goes,
Up the heathery mountain and down the rushy glen,
We daren't go a-hunting for Conor and his men.

There are few details remaining of how to play this archaic game, but it would appear that one child is chosen to stand in the centre of a circle while the rest hold hands and sing the song. When Annie Nelson is mentioned she joins Johnny in the centre of the circle. The couple enact the hugging and cuddling and the eating of the bridal cake. One version had as the last line: "And here's a clap, and here's a clap for Mrs (Nelson's) daughter", during which all players clapped hands.

3: And When I Die

We washed her, we dressed her, we rolled her in silk,
And we wrote down her name with a glass pen and ink.

Dear Annie, dear Annie, your true love is dead,
And we send you a letter to turn round your head.

Green Gravel

A very old and much-loved street game in Belfast, "Green Gravel" is a funeral game with a morbid sense of detail. The name of the game has prompted much debate on its meaning, but the general consensus is that it is derived from "green grave", meaning a freshly dug grave. All the rituals in the song are about the preparation of the remains for the burial: the washing, the dressing in silk (the shroud) and the memorial inscribed with a glass pen and ink. The words portray the death of someone very young, and the expression "to turn round your head" is used in children's songs to denote mourning. One of the earliest collection of versions of this game was in Manchester in 1837.

Green gravel, green gravel, your grass is so green,
You're the fairest young damsel that ever was seen.

We washed her, we dressed her, we rolled her in silk,
And we wrote down her name with a glass pen and ink.

(Dear Annie), (dear Annie), your true love is dead,
And we send you a letter to turn round your head.

The children form a ring, join hands and walk around singing the song. After the last line, the child whose name was mentioned in the penultimate line of the song turns completely around to face out of the ring. With her back to the centre of the ring, she joins hands with the players on each side as before and the game continues until another child's name is mentioned and he or she also turns and faces out of the ring. The game is complete when all the children have "turned" their backs to the centre of the ring.

Jenny Jo

The following version of this game was collected in Belfast by W. H. Patterson in 1891, but it was also played in Counties Louth and Waterford.

Jo is an old Scottish word for sweetheart and the game was first collected in Edinburgh in the 1820s. "Jenny Jo" is a curious mixture of a courting and funereal game followed by the resurrection of the dead. At one time, it was believed that too much mourning for the dead interfered with their rest, so the corpse rose to put an end to the mourning. With all the discussion of what colours to dress the remains in, it is hardly surprising that this is what happened.

It is extremely rare that children's games mention sectarian politics, as this one does with its references to Orangemen and croppies, who shaved their heads during the 1798 rebellion. The political references also indicate that this game was in existence in Ireland before 1820.

In other versions "black" represented the chimney sweeps; in Dublin "black" stood for the devil, while "blue" stood for the sailors.

The children form themselves into two parties. The first consists of Jenny Jo with her father and mother. Jenny Jo, who normally is a very small child, is concealed behind her parents. All the other children form the party of suitors who have come to visit Jenny Jo. They retire a short distance away, join hands, and then approach Jenny Jo's house singing:

> *We've come to court Jenny Jo,*
> *Jenny Jo, Jenny Jo,*
> *We've come to court Jenny Jo,*
> *Is she within?*

Something tragic has happened, the parents temporise and sing in reply:

> *Jenny Jo's washing clothes,*
> *Washing clothes, washing clothes,*
> *Jenny Jo's washing clothes,*
> *Can't see her today.*

The visiting party, still holding hands, walks backwards, singing:

> *Then fare ye well ladies-o,*
> *Ladies-o, ladies-o,*
> *Then fare ye well ladies,*
> *And gentlemen too.*

The visiting party returns immediately, singing as before; however, each time they are given an excuse by the parents: Jenny Jo is drying clothes, starching clothes, ironing clothes, until the parents finally announce the sad news:

> *Jenny Jo's lying dead,*
> *Lying dead, lying dead,*
> *Jenny Jo's lying dead,*
> *You can't see her today.*

The visiting party sings:

> *So, turn again, ladies-o,*
> *Ladies-o, ladies-o,*
> *So, turn again, ladies,*
> *And gentlemen too.*

Instead of returning home, the visiting party remains and sings:

> *What shall we dress her in,*
> *Dress her in, dress her in,*
> *What shall we dress her in,*
> *Shall it be red?*

The unhappy parents answer the question:

> *Red's for the soldiers,*
> *The soldiers, the soldiers,*
> *Red's for the soldiers,*
> *And that will not do.*

Various other colours are suggested but all are found to be unsuitable: black, because "black's for the mourners"; green, because "green's for the croppies"; orange, because "orange's for the orangemen". The song continues until white is suggested and the parents answer:

White's for the dead people,
The dead people, the dead people,
White's for the dead people,
And that will just do.

The parents then step aside to reveal Jenny Jo lying perfectly still on the ground. A hush falls on the visiting party. A funeral will have to be arranged and then suddenly Jenny Jo springs to life again and the game finishes with wild rejoicings.

Poor Toby Is Dead

Sometimes known as "Old Roger Is Dead", this is a funeral game in which the three main characters do not sing but merely act out the drama, while the "chorus" recounts the story. In folklore there is nothing unusual about planting rose bushes or trees at the head of a grave, as it was believed that the soul of the deceased passed into the tree or bush, thereby making it sacred. The old woman in the game was desecrating the grave by stealing the apples and is punished for her misdeed. She is generally thumped, slapped or given a clout. There are many ballads in the folk tradition which allude to this custom. The best known is "Barbara Allen":

> *The one was buried in the churchyard,*
> *And the other in the bower,*
> *And out of the one grew a red, red rose,*
> *And out of the other grew a briar.*

> *Poor Toby is dead and he lies in his grave,*
> *Lies in his grave, lies in his grave,*
> *Poor Toby is dead and he lies in his grave,*
> *Lies in his grave.*
>
> *We planted an apple tree over his head,*
> *Over his head, over his head,*
> *We planted an apple tree over his head,*
> *Over his head.*
>
> *When the apple trees were ripe and beginning to fall,*
> *Beginning to fall, beginning to fall,*
> *When the apple trees were ripe and beginning to fall,*
> *Beginning to fall.*

There came an old woman round picking them up,
Picking them up, picking them up,
There came an old woman round picking them up,
Picking them up.

Poor Toby got up and he gave her a kick,
Gave her a kick, gave her a kick,
Poor Toby got up and he gave her a kick,
Gave her a kick.

And the poor old woman went hippety hop,
Hippety hop, hippety hop,
And the poor old woman went hippety hop,
Hippety hop.

All the children form a circle around Toby, who is lying flat on his back in the centre. During the second verse one of the children goes into the centre of the circle and stands beside Toby to represent a tree. During the fourth verse another child approaches the centre and pretends to pick up the apples. During the fifth verse Toby jumps up and "beats" the old woman out of the circle. The old woman hobbles off pretending to be hurt, but the consolation prize is that she takes over Toby's role in the centre of the circle. The game continues as before.

Roman Soldiers

This song has echoes of the Roman invasion of Britain, but it has clearly become localised to Ireland. It is a game that was played until quite recently and was always found throughout Ireland in garrison towns such as Tipperary and Dublin. In the north-east of Ireland the melody and words were adapted by linen workers, who renamed it "Do You Want to Breed a Fight?" Scotland had its versions: "We Are King William's, King James's or Prince Charlie's Soldiers". The game thrives on the gory details of the injuries and the acting abilities of those injured to convey their mortal wounds.

Will you have a glass of wine?
Will you have a glass of wine?
Will you have a glass of wine?
We're the Irish soldiers.

No, we won't have a glass of wine,
No, we won't have a glass of wine,
No, we won't have a glass of wine,
We're the Roman soldiers.

Will you have a slice of cake?
Will you have a slice of cake?
Will you have a slice of cake?
We're the Irish soldiers.

No, we won't have a slice of cake,
No, we won't have a slice of cake,
No, we won't have a slice of cake,
We're the Roman soldiers.

Are you ready for a fight?
Are you ready for a fight?
Are you ready for a fight?
We're the Irish soldiers.

Or

Will you have a war with us?
Will you have a war with us?
Will you have a war with us?
We're the Irish soldiers.

Yes, we're ready for a fight,
Yes, we're ready for a fight,
Yes, we're ready for a fight,
We're the Roman soldiers.

Or

Yes, we'll have a war with you,
Yes, we'll have a war with you,
Yes, we'll have a war with you,
We're the Roman soldiers.

Irish Soldiers:

Shoot! Bang! Fire!

(Appropriate actions accompany each attack until all the Roman soldiers are lying down dead.)

Now we've only got one leg,
Now we've only got one leg,
Now we've only got one leg,
We're the Roman soldiers.

Irish Soldiers:

Shoot! Bang! Fire!

Now we've only got one eye,
Now we've only got one eye,
Now we've only got one eye,
We're the Roman soldiers.

Irish Soldiers:

Shoot! Bang! Fire!

Now we've only got one arm,
Now we've only got one arm,
Now we've only got one arm,
We're the Roman soldiers.

Irish Soldiers:

Shoot! Bang! Fire!

Now we've got no arms at all,
Now we've got no arms at all,
Now we've got no arms at all,
We're the Roman soldiers.

Irish Soldiers:

Shoot! Bang! Fire!

Now we're dead and in our graves,
Now we're dead and in our graves,
Now we're dead and in our graves,
We're the Roman soldiers.

Irish Soldiers:

Shoot! Bang! Fire!

Now we're all alive again,
Ready to fight and die again,
Now we're all alive again,
We're the Roman soldiers.

As many players as possible divide into equal sides and stand facing each other. Each side sings its verse as they advance and retire to and from each other. As the first "Shoot! Bang! Fire!" is uttered both sides stand still and point their right or left arms at each other as if they are holding guns; then they engage in battle. During the battle the Romans should illustrate their injuries with graphic gestures. After the fight is over they all form a ring and walk around, singing the last verse. After this the game recommences with the Irish soldiers playing the Roman soldiers.

Wallflowers

The first version of this game takes its first line from the game "Green Grass", but there the similarity ends. The reference to "stole away" indicates that the game is lamenting the loss of a child whom the fairies have taken away; the substitute child is recognised by her pale face. The expression "turn your face to the wall" appears in "Green Gravel" and is used in children's songs to indicate mourning. The game is played only by girls and is sung to the tune of "Nuts in May". In the second version of the game, mourning is again portrayed by the expression "turn your back to the wall". A version of this game from Waterford contains: "Turn your back to the game" as a last line.

> *Here we're set upon the green grass,*
> *Green grass, green grass,*
> *Here we're set upon the green grass,*
> *As green as any flower.*
>
> *(Mary Murry's) stole away,*
> *Stole away, stole away,*
> *(Mary Murry's) stole away,*
> *And lost her lily white flowers.*
>
> *It's well seen by her pale face,*
> *Pale face, pale face,*
> *It's well seen by her pale face,*
> *She may turn her face to the wall.*

Another version of "Wallflowers" is as follows:

Wallflowers, wallflowers, growing up so high,
All pretty children do not like to cry,
Except (Kitty O'Hare), she's the only one,
Oh fie for shame! Fie for shame!
Turn your back to the wall again.

The children form a ring, join hands and walk around, singing the song. After the last line, the child whose name was mentioned in the song turns completely around to face out of the ring. With her back to the centre of the ring, she joins hands with the players on each side as before and the game continues until another child's name is mentioned and he or she also turns and faces out of the ring. The game is finished when all the children have "turned" their backs to the centre of the ring.

4: Child's Play

I'm the wee melodie man,
The rumpty tumpty toddy man,
I always do the best I can,
To follow the wee melodie man.

Briar Rosebud

Better known as "Fair Rosa", this game recounts the story of Sleeping Beauty. Like "Poor Toby", the three main characters do not sing the song, but act out the drama while the "chorus" relates the story. It is interesting that one of the characters is called Fay, as the French word for fairy is "*fée*" and according to Sean O'Boyle in his book *The Irish Song Tradition*: "Most of the thematic material of Irish love songs both in Gaelic and in English seems to have originated in the songs of the troubadours of France." The imagery of a rose is not unusual in traditional songs and it is a clever device that can be used to convey innocence, with its beautifully coloured and scented flowers; however, prickly thorns lurking beneath the flower can also be used to convey evil.

The three main characters are chosen: Briar Rosebud, the Ugly Fay and Prince Charming. All the other players form a ring around Briar Rosebud, who preens herself in the centre of the circle; they all sing:

> *Briar Rosebud was a pretty child,*
> *A pretty child, a pretty child,*
> *Briar Rosebud was a pretty child,*
> *Long, long ago.*

During the next verse the children all raise their hands in the air:

> *She lived up in a lonely tower,*
> *A lonely tower, a lonely tower,*
> *She lived up in a lonely tower,*
> *Long, long ago.*

The wicked fairy, Ugly Fay, steps into the circle and they all sing:

> *One day there came an ugly Fay,*
> *An ugly Fay, an ugly Fay,*
> *One day there came an ugly Fay,*
> *Long, long ago.*

> *The ugly Fay gave her a rose,*
> *Gave her a rose, gave her a rose,*
> *The ugly Fay gave her a rose,*
> *Long, long ago.*

Ugly Fay joins the circle again.

> *She pricked her finger with the rose,*
> *With the rose, with the rose,*
> *She pricked her finger with the rose,*
> *Long, long ago.*

Briar Rosebud lies on the ground during the next verse.

> *She fell asleep for a hundred years,*
> *A hundred years, a hundred years,*
> *She fell asleep for a hundred years,*
> *Long, long ago.*

As the next verse is sung all the children crowd in around Briar Rosebud:

> *The briars grew thick around the tower,*
> *Around the tower, around the tower,*
> *The briars grew thick around the tower,*
> *Long, long ago.*

Prince Charming goes around the outside of the circle, pretending to ride his horse, and raises his arm in a cutting motion to break his way into the centre of the circle.

> *Prince Charming came and cut them down,*
> *Cut them down, cut them down,*
> *Prince Charming came and cut them down,*
> *Long, long ago.*

At this stage in some versions the players sing: "He took her hand and kissed it once." Prince Charming and Briar Rosebud both stand holding hands in the centre of the circle while the rest sing:

Briar Rosebud is now a happy bride,
A happy bride, a happy bride,
Briar Rosebud in now a happy bride,
Long, long ago.

The game can recommence with different players for the three main roles.

Loobey Light

This game is also known as "Lubin, Lubin", "Lubin Light" or "Loobey, Loobey", but whatever name it is called, it is one of the many examples of children's games that have been adapted and popularised by adults. It was recorded in 1941 by Jimmy Kennedy who sang it, complete with actions of course, as "The Okey Kokey". Since then, it has become the party game in which anybody, no matter what age group, can participate. At the end of the nineteenth century it was extremely popular with children, who could make the game last as long as possible by "putting in" as many parts of the anatomy as they could think of. The word "loobey" or "lubin" is derived from "looby", meaning a silly person or a lubber – a clumsy person – and judging by the antics of young or old who participate in this mime game, it is aptly titled!

Chorus:
Here we come looby, looby,
Here we come looby, light,
Here we come looby, looby,
All on a Saturday night.

Put all the right hands in,
Take all the right hands out,
Shake all the right hands together,
And turn yourselves about.

Chorus

Put all the left hands in,
Take all the left hands out,
Shake all the left hands together,
And turn yourselves about.

Chorus

Put all your right feet in,
Take all your right feet out,
Shake all your right feet together,
And turn yourselves about.

Chorus

Put all your left feet in,
Take all your left feet out,
Shake all your left feet together,
And turn yourselves about.

Chorus

Put all your heads in,
Take all your heads out,
Shake all your heads together,
And turn yourselves about.

Chorus

Put all the (Marys) in,
Take all the (Marys) out,
Shake all the (Marys) together,
And turn yourselves about.

Chorus

Put all yourselves in,
Take all yourselves out,
Shake all yourselves together,
And turn yourselves about.

Chorus

All the children form a ring and dance around, singing the first chorus. They stand still during the verses and as they sing they match their actions to the words. During the last line of each verse everybody turns completely around as quickly as they can. They continue to dance as they sing the chorus and stand still as they perform the actions during the verses.

Ma, Ma, Will You Buy?

This game is known throughout Great Britain. The game requires only two players for mother and son, who have a "grand conversation" about peeling and eating a banana. There is a love/hate scenario enacted with a colourful and colloquial last verse. It is not the only song in Belfast to have bananas as the topic: "We Have No Bananas" was popular during the depression of the 1930s and, of course, "Skinny malink melodeon long legs, big banana feet" is a very popular jingle with children. The first line is similar to "Milking Pail".

Ma, ma, will you buy me a
Will you buy me a, will you buy me a
Ma, ma, will you buy me a
Will you buy me a banana?

Yes, my son, I'll buy you a
I'll buy you a, I'll buy you a
Yes, my son, I'll buy you a
I'll buy you a banana.

Ma, ma, will you peel the skin
Will you peel the skin, will you peel the skin
Ma, ma, will you peel the skin
Of my lovely big banana?

Yes, my son, I'll peel the skin
Peel the skin, peel the skin
Yes, my son, I'll peel the skin
Of your lovely big banana.

Ma, ma, would you take a bite
Would you take a bite, would you take a bite
Ma, ma, would you take a bite
Of my lovely big banana?

Yes, my son, I'll take a bite
I'll take a bite, I'll take a bite
Yes, my son, I'll take a bite
Of your lovely big banana.

Ma, ma, you took too much
You took too much, you took too much
Ma, ma, you took too much
Of my lovely big banana.

Ma, ma, you're a dirty scut
You're a dirty scut, you're a dirty scut
Ma, ma, you're a dirty scut
You ate all my big banana.

Milking Pail

This is another game that was popular at the end of the last century, although milking pails had become outmoded and replaced by the more modern milking can. It was played widely in the countryside, where farmyard life was very familiar to children, and explains why the game was not popular in urban streets. The game predates the nineteenth century; one would have to be falling on very hard times to sell such a treasured possession as a feather bed, never mind such an important piece of equipment as a washing tub. In other versions collected in Britain the game becomes an accumulator with verses about the father or children sleeping in the pigsty or washing in a river or a thimble. Such were the luxuries of life on the farm!

Mother, will you buy me a milking can,
A milking can, a milking can?
Mother, will you buy me a milking can,
With my one, two and three?

Where will the money come from,
Come from, come from?
Where will the money come from,
With my one, two and three?

Sell our father's feather bed,
Feather bed, feather bed.
Sell our father's feather bed,
With my one, two and three.

Where shall father lie,
Father lie, father lie?
Where shall father lie,
With my one, two and three?

In the girls' bed,
The girls' bed, the girls' bed.
In the girls' bed,
With my one, two and three.

Where shall the girls lie,
Girls lie, girls lie?
Where shall the girls lie,
With my one, two and three?

In the boys' bed,
The boys' bed, the boys' bed.
In the boys' bed,
With my one, two and three.

Where shall the boys lie,
Boys lie, boys lie?
Where shall the boys lie,
With my one, two and three?

In the washing tub,
Washing tub, washing tub.
In the washing tub,
With my one, two and three.

The game can be played in two ways. In the first, one girl is chosen as the mother, while the rest of the children form a circle around her. They walk around and sing as they go. In the second, the mother stands facing a line of children, who advance and retire as the question and answer session proceeds.

The Wee Faloorie Man

I suspect that verses two and three have been added by some over-zealous bard, since they have no connection whatsoever with the first verse, which is similar to a much older song called "The Wee Melodie Man":

I'm the wee melodie man,
The rumpty tumpty toddy man,
I always do the best I can,
To follow the wee melodie man.

The song has been collected under various names: "I'm the Wee Polony Man", "The Gable Oary Man" and "The Holy Gabriel Man". One theory about the meaning of "Faloorie Man" is that it is derived from the Irish "fear leabhri", meaning the man of books, or chapman, who travelled around the countryside selling books or chapbooks. The game is a follow-the-leader game song where the children have to mimic exactly the actions of "The Melodie Man" – or pay the price!

I am the wee faloorie man,
A rattling roving Irishman,
I can do all that ever you can,
For I am the wee faloorie man.

I have a sister Mary Ann,
She washes her face with the frying pan,
Out she goes to hunt for a man,
I am the wee faloorie man.

I am a good old working man,
Each day I carry a wee tin can,
A large penny bap and a clipe of ham,
I am a good old working man.

In one version of this song all the children sit or stand in a circle; one is chosen as the Melodie Man to remain in the centre of the circle. The Melodie Man mimes the playing of an instrument and all the children have to mimic his actions. Of course, he will change instruments as quickly as he can to try and confuse his imitators. Whoever is late in following his actions goes into the centre. In another version, the Melodie Man again remains in the centre of the circle, surrounded by the children. Each of the children imitates the playing of an instrument, while he or she sings the song. Without any warning the Melodie Man may imitate any of the instruments being played in the circle and the players in the circle must immediately imitate the Melodie Man. If a player fails to do so, he or she takes the Melodie Man's place in the centre of the circle and the game continues as before.

There Was a Girl in Our School

All the nineteenth-century versions of this game vividly depict a woman's role. There are the usual verses about courting, marriage and the birth of children. Some versions, however, paint a bleaker picture, with verses about the loss of a baby, widowhood, being a washerwoman, scrubbing floors and cleaning. In some cases wife beating is described: "when my husband beat me" after which the husband's death is celebrated: "when my husband died … how happy was I." However, in later versions women's lot improves, with verses about women having careers as teachers, school mistresses and governesses.

There was a girl in our school,
In our school, in our school,
There was a girl in our school,
And this is the way she went.
And this is the way she went.

Then she became a lady,
A lady, a lady,
Then she became a lady,
And this is the way she went.
And this is the way she went.

Then she became a teacher,
A teacher, a teacher,
Then she became a teacher,
And this is the way she went.
And this is the way she went.

Then she got married,
Married, married,
Then she got married,
And this is the way she went.
And this is the way she went.

Then she got a baby,
A baby, a baby,
Then she got a baby,
And this is the way she went.
And this is the way she went.

Then the baby died,
Died, died,
Then the baby died,
And this is the way she went.
And this is the way she went.

Then she got a donkey,
A donkey, a donkey,
Then she got a donkey,
And this is the way she went.
And this is the way she went.

Then the donkey kicked her,
Kicked her, kicked her,
Then the donkey kicked her,
And this is the way she went.
And this is the way she went.

Then she went to hospital,
To hospital, to hospital,
Then she went to hospital,
And this is the way she went.
And this is the way she went.

Then she was sewing,
Sewing, sewing,
Then she was sewing,
And this is the way she went.
And this is the way she went.

Then the needle pricked her,
Pricked her, pricked her,
Then the needle pricked her,
And this is the way she went.
And this is the way she went.

Then she died,
She died, she died,
Then she died,
And this is the way she went.
And this is the way she went.

The children form a ring and join hands. They all dance or walk around while singing the first three lines of each verse. Then they all stand still, unclasp hands and sing the last two lines of each verse. As they do so, they mime some action to illustrate what they are singing about. They all join hands again and sing the first three lines of the next verse as they walk or dance around.

To illustrate a lady, players might hold their dresses and walk daintily around. As a teacher, they can hold up a finger to silence the child beside them or pretend to smack them with a cane. For marriage they can walk around arm in arm with the child beside them. During verse five they can pretend to rock the baby in their arms and cry when the baby dies. Later they can shout at and beat the child beside them like a donkey.

The success of the game depends on how good the children are at improvising the actions to indicate what or whom they are singing about.

5: Underneath the Arches

In and out the dusty bluebells,
In and out the dusty bluebells,
In and out the dusty bluebells,
I'll be your master.

Dusty Bluebells

There is a striking contrast of image between the bluebell, with its delicate shade of blue, and the dusty air of the city in the words of this game, which is one of the most popular street games played today. No other versions were collected during the nineteenth century, although "Dusty Bluebells" is similar to "Round about the Ladies", from which it has borrowed and adapted the second verse. As the children sing "tipper ripper rapper" there is more thumping than patting, and as the players hold onto each other, while threading their way through the arches, many a skirt and pair of trousers are pulled down in the fray. Dublin, of course, has its variation:

Follow me to the dear old Dublin,
Follow me to the dear old Dublin,
Follow me to the dear old Dublin,
Early in the morning.

In and out the dusty bluebells,
In and out the dusty bluebells,
In and out the dusty bluebells,
I'll be your master.

Tipper ripper rapper on your shoulder,
Tipper ripper rapper on your shoulder,
Tipper ripper rapper on your shoulder,
I'll be your master.

Follow me to Londonderry,
Follow me to Londonderry,
Follow me to Londonderry,
I'll be your master.

Tipper ripper rapper on your shoulder,
Tipper ripper rapper on your shoulder,
Tipper ripper rapper on your shoulder,
I'll be your master.

The children form a circle, join hands and raise them in the air to create a circle of arches. One player is chosen, who then weaves in and out of the formed arches, while the rest of the children sing the first verse. When they finish singing, the chosen player stops behind one of the children forming an arch and starts to tap on his or her shoulder, while the rest of the children begin to sing the second verse. The player who has been tapped detaches himself from the circle of arches and links on behind the chosen player. They both start to weave in and out of the arch, while the rest of the children sing the first verse as before. Another child is tapped, or in many cases "thumped" on the shoulder, while the rest of the children sing the second verse. This child then links onto the other two players, and the three children continue to weave through the arches. The game continues with the circle of arches getting smaller and the line becoming longer.

Here Are the Robbers

Also known as "See" or "Hark, the Robber's Coming Through", this game enacts the capture of a robber, with the moral that if you steal you will have to be punished by going to jail. Its infectious melody was so popular that its lyrics often were grafted onto "London Bridge" by singing: "What has this poor prisoner done?" Since both songs share the same melody and the refrain "My Fair Lady", this is hardly surprising. "Here Are the Robbers" was also incorporated in "Oranges and Lemons". In the Dublin version of the game an intoned chorus is added to the end of the game, similar to the lines in "Oranges and Lemons":

> *Chip chop*
> *Chip chop*
> *The last man's head is OFF.*

One word is spoken to each child and is accompanied by the chopping actions of the arched arms, descending like a falling axe to decapitate one of the player's heads, as in a sacrificial killing. "Off" is spoken with great forcefulness. The first verse of the song has sometimes been sung mischievously during church collections.

> *Here are the robbers coming through,*
> *Coming through, coming through,*
> *Here are the robbers coming through,*
> *My fair lady.*
>
> *What did the robbers do to you?*
> *Do to you, do to you?*
> *What did the robbers do to you?*
> *My fair lady.*
>
> *Stole my watch and stole my chain,*
> *Stole my watch and stole my chain,*
> *Stole my watch and stole my chain,*
> *My fair lady.*
>
> *Then you must go to jail,*
> *Go to jail, go to jail,*
> *Then you must go to jail,*
> *My fair lady.*

Two children join hands and raise them to form an arch; the rest of the children file under, singing as they go. After the last verse one of the children is sent as a prisoner to jail, behind one of the two children forming the arch. Sometimes the prisoner is asked: "Which will you have? A golden apple or a golden pear?" Depending on the answer, the prisoner falls in behind one of the two children forming the arch. The game begins again and continues until all the children end up behind one or other of the two children who form the arch. The game ends with a tug of war. In another version of the game the children form two lines and sing the first four verses of the song as above. The robbers defiantly walk between the two lines and ask:

> *How many pounds will set us free?*
> *Set us free, set us free?*
> *How many pounds will set us free?*
> *My fair lady.*
>
> *One hundred pounds will set you free,*
> *Will set you free, will set you free,*
> *One hundred pounds will set you free,*
> *My fair lady.*
>
> *We have not got a hundred pounds,*
> *A hundred pounds, a hundred pounds,*
> *We have not got a hundred pounds,*
> *My fair lady.*
>
> *Then to prison you must go,*
> *You must go, you must go,*
> *Then to prison you must go,*
> *My fair lady.*
>
> *Then to prison we will not go,*
> *We will not go, we will not go,*
> *Then to prison we will not go,*
> *My fair lady.*

When the robbers have sung this reply they run away, to be quickly chased by the two lines of children who capture them and put them in prison.

How Many Miles to Babylon

In Great Britain Babylon has been adapted to Bethlehem, Banbury and Barley Bridge, but in Ireland it has been localised to Barney Bridge. The game is similar to and, in some instances, grafted onto "Thread the Needle", which diminished in popularity as this game prospered during the nineteenth century. Some versions have: "Let King George and his family through", which indicates the age of the game and also accounts for the children curtseying before they hurl themselves headlong under the arch.

How many miles to Barney's Bridge?
Three score and ten.
Will I be there at Candlemas?
Yes, and back again.
Open your gates and let us through.
Not without a beck and boo.
There's the beck, there's the boo
Open your gates and let us through.

The children form a semi-circle and the two tallest stand at each end. They all hold hands. The two children at one end ask the questions by singing the uneven lines, while the two children at the other end answer the questions by singing the even lines. At the last line the children who have been answering the questions hold their hands up in the air to form a bridge. All the other children rush headlong under the arch, still holding hands.

In the Belfast version the last line of the game is "Yes, but take care of the hindmost man", after which the children who have formed the arch drop their hands over one of the children filing under and take a prisoner, who then stands behind one or other of the children forming the arch. The game continues until all the children have been captured.

The Louth, Dublin and Belfast versions generally end with "Oranges and Lemons". The Louth version has "Here's my black" (raising one foot) and "Here's my blue" (raising the other).

London Bridge

This game is universally known and the details rarely change: the bridge is always falling down and rebuilt in a particular manner, and the game always ends by taking captives. "London Bridge" has never been renamed after any bridges in Ireland. It is similar to "Oranges and Lemons" and "Here Are the Robbers", which has the same melody and refrain of "My Fair Lady". The Cork version has "Lime and stone would waste away" and continues with:

> *Build it up with penny loaves,*
> *Penny loaves would be eaten away.*
> *Built it up with silver and gold,*
> *Silver and gold would be stolen away.*
> *Get a man to watch all night …*

It was first published in a children's book in 1744.

> *London Bridge is broken down,*
> *Broken down, broken down,*
> *London Bridge is broken down,*
> *My fair lady.*
>
> *Stones and lime will build it up,*
> *Build it up, build it up,*
> *Stones and lime will build it up,*
> *My fair lady.*
>
> *Get a man to watch all night,*
> *Watch all night, watch all night,*
> *Get a man to watch all night,*
> *My fair lady.*
>
> *Perhaps that man might fall asleep,*
> *Fall asleep, fall asleep,*
> *Perhaps that man might fall asleep,*
> *My fair lady.*

Get a dog to watch all night,
Watch all night, watch all night,
Get a dog to watch all night,
My fair lady.

If that dog should run away,
Run away, run away,
If that dog should run away,
My fair lady.

Give that dog a bone to pick,
A bone to pick, a bone to pick,
Give that dog a bone to pick,
My fair lady.

Two children join hands and raise them in the air to form an arch. The other children form a line and hold onto each other's dresses or waists and run under the arch, singing the uneven verses. The two children who have formed the arch sing the even verses. The game continues until all the children have had their turn forming the arch.

There are various refrains for the fourth line, such as "Grand says the little bee" or "Grand says the little dee".

Oranges and Lemons

This is one of the most enduring children's games, and was first collected in 1744. It has always been played and sung with its original London place names and has never been adapted to include Irish names. The climax is violent and dramatic as each child is taken prisoner. It is a similar arch game to "London Bridge" and "Here Are the Robbers".

Bells had a very important function in village life. They were rung to warn the inhabitants of approaching danger or to call them together for a meeting; if a prisoner was being led through the streets for a public execution, the sound of bells would ring out.

Oranges and lemons,
Say the bells of St Clement's;
You owe me five farthings,
Say the bells of St Martin's;
When will you pay me?
Say the bells of Old Bailey;
When I grow rich,
Say the bells of Shoreditch;
When will that be?
Say the bells of Stepney;
I'm sure I don't know,
Says the Great Bell of Bow.

Spoken:

Here comes a candle to light you to bed
AND HERE COMES A CHOPPER TO CHOP OFF YOUR HEAD
THE LAST, LAST, LAST, LAST MAN'S HEAD!

Two of the tallest children stand facing each other and form an arch. One player is called Orange, the other is called Lemon. The other players form a line, hold onto each other by the waist or shoulders and go under the arch and around Orange the first time. The second time they go around Lemon. All the while they sing the verses. The last three lines are spoken very slowly and emphatically by Orange and Lemon. When they reach the word "head" at the end of the second line, they drop their arms and trap one of the children and ask him if he wants to be Orange or Lemon. The captive decides, stands behind the chosen one and holds him by the waist. The game continues until all the children are arranged behind Orange and Lemon. Then there is a tug-o-war until one of the parties falls down or is pulled over a given mark.

The Grand Old Duke of York

This game has been adopted from the song "The King of France", which was known as far back as the early 1600s:

The King of France went up the hill
With forty thousand men,
The King of France came down the hill
And ne'er went up again.

It was unfortunate that Frederick, Duke of York, came under the scrutiny of historians; they made a laughing stock of him, and to add insult to injury he has been lampooned in this children's game. It is not the most flattering way to remember somebody who was an extremely competent commander-in-chief.

Oh, the grand old Duke of York
He had ten thousand men,
He marched them up to the top of the hill
And he marched them down again.
And when they were up, they were up
And when they were down, they were down,
And when they were only half way up
They were neither up nor down.

The children arrange themselves into two lines with the boys facing the girls. The song is sung once and as the players begin to sing it the second time, the first boy in the line takes the hand of the first girl and leads her down the centre of the two lines and back up to the top again. The couple separate and the boy marches around to the back of the boys' line, while the girl marches around to the back of the girls' line. Each is followed by their respective lines of boys and girls as they file in behind. As the first girl and boy meet at the end of the line they join hands and raise them in the air to form an arch. All the other children pass under the arch in pairs. The second boy and girl in the line commence the game again and so it continues until all the children have had their chance to lead.

6: Catch Me If You Can

Hurley burley trumpa trace
The cow ran from the market place.
Some go far and some go near
Where shall this poor Frenchman steer?

Brogey Mor

This game was popular around the 1850s. The melody is better known as the instrumental tune "The Rose Tree", which Thomas Moore also used for his song "I'd Mourn the Hopes that Leave Me" and is still widely played in music sessions throughout Ireland. Several versions of the game have been collected in Ulster but all are known as "Brogey Mor", which is Irish for "big shoe". Other nicknames used during the game are "Paddy Whack" or "Tangle O' Wrack".

Lay on him, Brogey Mor
With yer fa-re-a-raddy-o,
And likewise, Singey Gore
With yer fa-re-a-raddy-o.

Lay on him, Pot and Pan
With yer fa-re-a-raddy-o,
Take off him everyone
With yer fa-re-a-raddy-o.

Lay on him, oul' Grey Rat
With yer fa-re-a-raddy-o,
Take off him, Brogey Mor
With yer fa-re-a-raddy-o.

Lay on him everyone
With yer fa-re-a-raddy-o,
Take off him, Pot and Pan
With yer fa-re-a-raddy-o.

The first boy stands with his back to the wall. A second boy stoops and puts his head against the chest of the first boy. The rest of the children stand around the stooped boy. Each child is given a name, such as Brogey Mor, Singey Gore, Oul' Grey Rat and Pot and Pan. The first boy begins to sing and the rest of the children join in. They must follow their instructions to either "lay on" or "take off" their fists on the back of the stooped boy, while keeping time to the music. If any of them makes the mistake of "laying on" when they should be "taking off", they have to take the place of the stooping boy. Generally, this game turns into a good thumping match rather than a "laying on" of fists!

Carry My Lady to London

This is a very simple children's game with no known melody surviving, probably because the quatrain was intoned and not sung. In England at the beginning of this century, some areas had pin shows, where buttercups and daisies were displayed between two sheets of glass and wrapped in brown paper. The owner of the flowers had a rhyme: "Give me a pin to stick under my chin", and when he was paid some money, the flowers were unwrapped and displayed to the purchaser.

Whatever the real meaning of the phrase, you can be sure that the passenger had a rough ride on the seat as the carriers hurtled along the streets as fast as they could go.

Give me a pin to stick in my thumb
To carry my lady to London,
Give me another to stick in my other
To carry her a little bit farther.

Two children cross hands and hold each other by the wrists to form a seat, on which a child can sit and be carried around. As they carry the child they recite the quatrain.

Draw a Pail of Water

Of the fifteen versions of the game collected by A. B. Gomme in the 1880s, only two mention oaten bread: one from Belfast and one from *Halliwell's Nursery Rhymes and Games*, first published in 1842. All the others contain the first line after which the game is called: "Draw a pail of water for my lady's daughter". The words are very obscure and their meaning has long since been lost.

Draw a pail of water for my lady's daughter,
Her father's a King, her mother's a Queen,
Her two little sisters are dressed in green.
Stamping grass and parsley,
Marigold leaves and daisies,
Give a golden ring and a silver pin.
Sift the lady's oaten meal, sift it into flour,
Put it in a chest of drawers and let it lie an hour.
One of my rush,
Two of my rush,
Please, young lady, come under the bush.
My bush is too high, my bush is too low,
Please, young lady, come under my bough.
Draw a pail of water for a lady's daughter,
Her father's a King, her mother's a Queen,
Her two little sisters are dressed in green.

Two girls face each other and hold each other by both hands. Another two girls face each other and also hold each other by both hands across the other two, forming a cross. They see-saw backwards and forwards as they sing the song. As they sing "One of my rush, two of my rush" they lift their criss-crossed arms in the air and one of the other children runs under. They bring their arms down again to trap the child. The game is repeated until four children have been caught in the criss-crossed arms.

Grannie's Needle

Sometimes known as "Hen and Chicken" or "Fox and Goose", all versions of this game contain the same format of a question and answer session followed by the mayhem of Grannie chasing after the chickens. There is no melody for this game, but there is a gradual build-up to the climax of the last line, which Grannie intones with a blood-curdling scream. All versions generally mimic the pursuit and capture of animals on the farm.

> *What are you looking for, Granny?*
> *My Granny's needle.*
> *What are you going to do with the needle, Granny?*
> *To make a bag.*
> *And what are you going to do with the bag, Granny,*
> *To gather sand.*
> *And what are you going to do with the sand, Granny?*
> *To sharpen knives.*
> *And what are you going to do with the knives, Granny?*
> *To cut off chickens' heads.*

All the children stand in a line, one behind the other. A leader is chosen to stand at the front of the line. Another child is chosen as the outsider and pretends to scratch the ground. The leader asks the questions and the outsider answers them. The outsider tries to dodge past the leader to catch one of the children in the line, while the leader defends the line and prevents any of the children from being captured. The outsider finally catches one of the children, who then becomes the outsider. The game continues as before.

Hot Cockles

This game, which was generally played at Christmas, was collected by a Miss Keane in Cork in the 1880s. It was played as follows. A player has a handkerchief tied over his eyes by one of the other participants, who leads him to a chair and makes him kneel with his forehead resting on the seat of the chair. The kneeling player has one of his hands placed on his back with the palm facing upwards. The other players give him a slap on the hand and he has to guess who is hitting him. If he guesses correctly, the named player is then blindfolded and the game continues as before. Versions of this game were collected in England as early as 1640.

Hurley Burley

"Hurley Burley" is another game that is not sung but has plenty of scope for three players to "gulder" at the top of their voices. The use of the Frenchman is interesting, since that would date the song back to the 1790s when a French army was expected in Ireland to fight against the English. The game always had a painful ending and many a time the ground was carpeted with skin and hair!

A boy stands with his back to the wall, while a second boy stoops and puts his head against the chest of the first boy. A third boy, who is the leader, stands behind the stooped boy. The leader recites the following:

Hurley burley trumpa trace,
The cow ran from the market place.
Some go far and some go near,
Where shall this poor Frenchman steer?

In answer to the question the stooping boy tells him to go to (Paddy Gaw's corner). The Frenchman goes to this position about fifty yards away. The verse is repeated and another boy is sent to (Wilson's grocery), and yet another is sent to (Eakin's entry), and so on until all the boys have been sent to different locations. The leader then shouts, "Are you all in your places?" and waits for their replies. When they are all ready he shouts, "Hurley home, hurley home, hurley home." All the boys race back to see who gets "home" first. The last one home is surrounded by the rest. They all take a lock of his hair and recite the following:

Rannell him, Dick,
Catch him, Davey,
All the men three score and ten,
Anyone not at the rannelling match
Will be rannelled over again.
Heigh ho, buttermilk oh,
Short pluck or large draw.

If the unfortunate victim answers "short pluck", they all give his hair a pluck and then release him.

Johnny Hairy, Crap In

This is a game with a most unusual title that was collected in Leitrim in 1892 by a Mr Duncan; it is also a very rare example of a game that has metamorphosed from the Irish language into English. "Crap in" is derived from the Irish "*Crap isteach*", meaning to draw in. The game has the same first two lines as "Hurley Burley" and has the common feature of guessing games and riddle rhymes: if the wrong answer is given by one of the players he or she is punished by the kicks or thumps of the other players. The game has three distinct strands: forfeits (kneeling), blindfolding (blind man's bluff) and guessing. It is played as follows.

All the players sit around the fire and stick their right foot out. The master of the game recites:

> *One-ery, two-ery, dickery dary,*
> *Wispy, spindy, smoke of the kindy,*
> *Old Johnny Hairy, Crap In!*

Each word is directed at every player individually and whoever has "Crap In!" said to him has to draw in his right foot. The game continues until all feet are drawn in, except for those of the last player. This player has to kneel down and is then blindfolded. The master of the game places his elbow on the player's back and hits him either with his elbow or his fist, saying:

> *Hurley burley trump the trace,*
> *The cow ran through the market place.*
> *Simon alley hunt the buck,*
> *How many horns stand up?*

At the same time as he recites the last line, he holds up several fingers for all to see, while the player kneeling has to guess. If he is lucky and guesses correctly the master takes his place. If he guesses incorrectly another player comes and "bates" him on the back. The game commences as before – just the sort of thing for long winter nights!

Relievio

This is a very similar game to "Grannie's Needle" as its sole aim is taking captives. One child is chosen as captor to chase after all the other children and to take prisoners. The prisoner joins hands with the captor and the two of them chase after the rest of the children, capturing as many prisoners as possible. The game continues until they have all joined hands and become prisoners.

In other versions of the game two teams are formed and an area called a den is decided upon where captives are jailed. One team appoints a guard for the den, while the rest of the players have to run off and pursue captives. The game begins when the other team has run off to hide, shouting: "Re-lie-vee-o". The captives are brought back and imprisoned in the den and can only be freed if one of their own members runs through the den without being caught, while triumphantly shouting: "Re-lie-vee-o". All those captured in the den are free to run away and the game continues until all the children are captured and put in the den.

This was a game that was popular in the wide open spaces of the countryside, but a Dublin skipping game refers to it as well.

Down in the alley-o,
Where we played Relievi-o,
Up comes her mother-o,
Have you seen my Mary-o?
Why did you let her go?
Because she bit my finger-o,
Which finger did she bite?
The little finger on the right.

7: Spring Has Sprung!

Here we come gathering nuts in May,
Nuts in May, nuts in May,
Here we come gathering nuts in May,
May, May, May.

The Mulberry Bush

"The Mulberry Bush" is another of the most popular children's games, in which the action of the story is related through mime. Earlier versions of the game are centred on the theme of personal hygiene, but later versions embody domesticity and education. The action of the game generally took place on Mayday around the May Bush. This did not got unnoticed by Brand in 1875, when he wrote: "in Ireland men and women dance around about a bush in a large ring". The game is sung to the tune of "Nuts in May" and was first noted in 1760.

Chorus:
Here we go round the Mulberry Bush,
Here we go round the Mulberry Bush,
Here we go round the Mulberry Bush,
On a cold and frosty morning.

This is the way we wash our clothes,
This is the way we wash our clothes,
This is the way we wash our clothes,
On a cold and frosty morning.

Chorus

This is the way we iron our clothes,
This is the way we iron our clothes,
This is the way we iron our clothes,
On a cold and frosty morning.

Chorus

This is the way we wash our face,
This is the way we wash our face,
This is the way we wash our face,
On a cold and frosty morning.

Chorus

This is the way we brush our hair,
This is the way we brush our hair,
This is the way we brush our hair,
On a cold and frosty morning.

The song can continue with many other verses, such as: wash our hands, bake our bread, sweep the floor, go to school.

All the children form a circle, hold hands and dance around, singing the chorus. During the last line of the chorus they stop holding hands and quickly turn completely around and then stand still. The children start singing the verses and miming the actions until the last line, when they quickly turn completely around, join hands and start singing as they dance around again.

Nuts in May

This game is universally known and heralds in the "merrie month of May". It does, however, pose the question: when did anybody ever pick nuts in May? The answer is never, since the word "nuts" is a misspelling of the old Anglo-Irish word "knots", meaning posies or bunches of flowers or bushes. These knots were picked by children on Mayday to decorate the May Pole, the doors of houses or to "make the May Bush" around which children gathered on Mayday to play games and to dance.

This is probably the most popular and widely played of singing games, whose melody has been borrowed many times for other songs. The refrain is sometimes sung as "Cold and frosty morning" or "So early in the morning". It was first noted around 1760.

Here we come gathering nuts in May,
Nuts in May, nuts in May,
Here we come gathering nuts in May,
May, May, May.

Who will you have for nuts in May,
Nuts in May, nuts in May,
Who will you have for nuts in May,
May, May, May?

(Bessie Stewart) for nuts in May,
Nuts in May, nuts in May,
(Bessie Stewart) for nuts in May,
May, May, May.

Very well, so you may,
So you may, so you may,
Very well, so you may,
May, May, May.

Whom will you have to take her away,
Take her away, take her away,
Whom will you have to take her away,
Way, way, way?

(Joe McClurg) to take her away,
To take her away, to take her away,
(Joe McClurg) to take her away,
Way, way, way.

The children form two lines of equal length and face each other. Enough space is left in between the two lines to enable them to walk backwards and forwards as each line sings its verse. One line sings the odd verses, while the other sings the even verses. Occasionally, at the end of the fifth verse, a handkerchief is laid on the ground or a mark is made on the ground. The two children named during the game take each other's right hand and try to pull each other over the handkerchief or the mark. The idea is to pull the other person over to the other side. The child who has been pulled across becomes the "captured nut" and joins the other line. The game begins again with one side now singing the odd verses and the other side singing the even.

Thread the Needle

Like some versions of "How Many Miles to Babylon", this game actually refers to King George, which gives a general indication of when the game was popular. In fact, it even predates this era; a fresco in the town hall of Sienna in Tuscany painted by Ambrogio Lorenzetti (1319–48) depicts women playing this very game. In Poor Robin's Almanac of 1738 it states: "the summer quarter follows Spring as close as girls do one another, when playing 'Thread-my-Needle'." The game was associated with springtime, and in some cases whole villages participated in the frolics. It has similarities to "How Many Miles to Babylon" and "The Big Ship Sails".

Open your gates as wide as high
And let King George's horses by,
For the night is dark and we cannot see
But thread your long needle and sew.

All the children stand in two rows and each child holds the hands of the opposite player. The last two children in the rows form an arch by raising their hands in the air. As they sing the song, the rest of the children run under the arch. When they have all passed beneath the arch, the first pair who went under now forms the arch for the others to go through. The game continues until each pair has formed the arch.

The Big Ship Sails

There were no versions of this game collected during the last century under this name, but "The Big Ship Sails" is very closely related to an old game called "Wind Up the Bush Faggot", in which children formed a long line and held hands. The tallest child was chosen as a pivot, around which the rest of the children slowly circled, forming a tight coil and singing as they went, like a snake wrapping itself around a tree. The children continued singing as the coil unwound. It is hardly surprising then that in older forms this game was called "The Serpent's Coil", "Snail's Creep" or "Wind Up the Watch".

The following was noted in *Wilde's Ancient Cures, Charms and Usages of Ireland*:

> On May day in Ireland, all the young men and maidens hold hands
> and dance in a circle … moving in curves from right to left as if
> imitating the windings of a serpent.

The only difference in "The Big Ship" is that an arch or alley is formed. Apart from this, the month varies between 14 November or 14 December.

The big ship sails on the alley alley-o,
The alley alley-o, the alley alley-o,
The big ship sails on the alley alley-o,
On the last day of September.

One of the children stands, as leader, with a hand against the wall and raises it to form an arch or alley. All the others form a line behind the leader and hold hands. The first one in the line takes the leader's free hand. The players start to sing and the child at the other end of the line from the leader makes her way through the arch formed by the leader. The players continue to sing the verse and file under the arch until the whole line has become woven into a tight circular knot. During the last line they all put their hands up in the air and the "knot" breaks up with much hilarity. Alternatively, they can unravel – as in the older form of the game – as they sing the verse again.

The May Queen

There is an old country saying: "April showers bring forth May flowers", but May time in Belfast brought much more; the streets were thronged with spectators during the arrival of the May queens and their courtiers. These were children who dressed up to welcome in the month of May. The May Queen had pride of place and was usually dressed in her mother's discarded clothing, high heels and a veil made out of old lace curtains adorned with mayflowers. She was transported around the streets on the royal coach, which was a go-chair or cart suitably adorned with a patchwork quilt and mayflowers. The Queen's retinue were also dressed up in whatever costumes they could lay their hands on. Their faces were often blackened with burnt cork or soot, hence the frequent reference to "darkie" in their songs. Their sole aim was to collect money in their little red boxes and passers-by were often accosted by the pert question: "Anyfin' for the Quane av the May, mister?" They were not to be refused! Ladies did not escape their notice either and a more subtle form of attack was used when they sang an adopted version of "Lady on the Mountain":

> *Lady, you have gold and silver,*
> *Lady, you have a house and land,*
> *Lady, you have ships on the ocean,*
> *All I want is a penny if you can!*

Inevitably, with so many queens roaming the streets, there were confrontations between rival factions, and each taunted the other with their queen's great exploits, such as being able to birl her leg or eat a hard bap. Many a time, the day ended in fisticuffs. Nevertheless, Mayday had been well and truly welcomed in.

Our Queen up the river with her yah, yah, yah,
Our Queen up the river with her yah, yah, yah,
Our Queen up the river and we'll keep her there forever,
With her yah, yah, yah, yah, yah.

The other Queen down the river with her boo, boo, boo,
The other Queen down the river with her boo, boo, boo,
The other Queen down the river and we'll keep her there forever,
With her boo, boo, boo, boo, boo.

Our Queen can tumble a pole, tumble a pole, tumble a pole,
Our Queen can tumble a pole, tumble a pole.

Our Queen can birl her leg, birl her leg, birl her leg,
Our Queen can birl her leg, birl her leg.

Our Queen can smoke a fag, smoke a fag, smoke a fag,
Our Queen can smoke a fag, smoke a fag.

Our Queen can ate a hard bap, ate a hard bap, ate a hard bap,
Our Queen can ate a hard bap, ate a hard bap.

Our Queen can ate a currant loaf, ate a currant loaf,
  ate a currant loaf,
Our Queen can ate a currant loaf, ate a currant loaf.

Our Queen up the river with her yah, yah, yah,
Our Queen up the river with her yah, yah, yah,
Our Queen up the river and we'll keep her there forever,
With her yah, yah, yah, yah, yah.

The other Queen down the river with her boo, boo, boo,
The other Queen down the river with her boo, boo, boo,
The other Queen down the river and we'll keep her there forever,
With her boo, boo, boo, boo, boo.

Queen of the May

At the beginning of the last century, Mayday was a holiday for chimney sweeps. They were a colourful sight parading through the streets. In 1824 their antics were described in Dublin by Andrew Bigelow of Massachusetts: "They deck themselves … on the present occasion with figured paper caps and ornaments and patrol the sidewalks soliciting season-pence from every passenger." This is exactly what the May queens were still doing on our city streets over a century and a half later. During the 1800s it was normal practice to use young children for cleaning chimneys and inevitably their faces were blackened with soot for the Mayday celebrations. This explains why these songs have references to "the darkie".

To be the Queen of the May,
To be the Queen of the May,
To welcome (Maggie Murphy, Murphy, Murphy),
To welcome (Maggie Murphy),
To be the Queen of the May.

Heigh-ho, bravo, our Queen won,
Our Queen won,
Heigh-ho, bravo, our Queen won.

The darkie said he'd marry her,
Marry her, marry her,
The darkie said he'd marry her,
Because she was the Queen.
Because she was the Queen, because she was the Queen,
The darkie said he'd marry her,
Marry her, marry her,
The darkie said he'd marry her, because she was the Queen.

Heigh-ho, bravo, our Queen won,
Our Queen won,
Heigh-ho, bravo, our Queen won.

8: You Are Out!

Picking and Choosing Games

O-U-T spells out
And out you must go!

Eenio, meenie, miney mo,
Catch a tigger by the toe,
If he squeals, let him go,
Eenie, meenie, miney mo!

This is one of the most widely known counting rhymes today, and yet it was also very well known in the 1880s throughout Ireland. It is another example of a rhyming game which depends on the use of nonsensical words for its rhythm. Another form of the game is the use of numbers, the alphabet or spelling within the rhyme. Most versions have the word "out" at or near the end, so that the player on whom the word "falls" knows she has to leave the game and wait until the next one starts.

Donald Duck and Mickey Mouse,
Built a house under the sea,
Said Donald Duck to Mickey Mouse,
What number shall it be?

The player pointed to selects any number, for example number 7, and takes up the count.

One-two-three-four-five-six-seven-OUT!

One other example of this game uses a straightforward, coherent rhyming narrative.

Snowflakes, snowflakes, falling down,
Falling on children running around,
Please, little snowflake, have no doubt,
Fall on a child and that child is out.

Both boys and girls can participate in these games and no matter what form the game takes, the procedure for playing it rarely varies. One child stands facing the rest of the children in a line; or all children form a circle around one player. The "chosen" child recites the rhymes in a monotone voice, but pays particular attention to the rhythmical metre of the lines. The player points to each child individually, as well as to herself, and intones one word of the rhyme per person. Whomever the last word falls upon is "on it" and can take pride of place in the centre of the circle or face the line of children in order to perform the choosing ritual. Alternatively, that player is "out" and must leave the circle or the line and wait until all the rest are out. The last remaining child who has not been called out is "on it".

The following four rhymes were collected during the 1880s.

Eena, deena, dina, dass,
Bottle a weena, wina, wass,
Pin, pan, muska, dan,
Eedleum, deedleum, twenty-one,
Eery, ory, OUT goes she!

One-ery, two-ery, dickery, davy,
Hallabone, crackabone, tenery, navy,
Linkum, tinkum, merrycum can,
Halibo, crackery, twenty-one.

Mitty Matty had a hen,
She lays white eggs for gentlemen,
Gentlemen come every day,
Mitty Matty runs away.
Hi-ho, who is at home?
Father, Mother, Jumping Joan,
O-U-T, out,
Take off the latch and walk out!

Hiddlety, diddlety, dumpty,
The cat ran up the plum tree,
Send a hack to fetch her back,
Hiddlety, diddlety, dumpty.

Here are several other rhymes.

Twenty-one, pick a chum.

Children count to twenty-one and the last one pointed to is out.

One, two, sky blue
All out by you.

Ingle, angle, silver bangle,
Ingle, angle, out.

O-U-T spells out
And out you must go!

Ibble, obble,
Black bottle,
Ibble, obble out!

Ibble, obble, black bottle,
Ibble, obble out,
Turn a dirty dishcloth
Inside out!

A man lit his pipe
And it went out!

Pig's snout,
Walk straight out!

Each peach, pear, plum,
Pick out your very best chum!

Child pointed to selects chum, for example, Louise, and continues.

L-O-U-I-S-E spells Louise and
Out you must go!

Turn to the East and turn to the West,
And turn to the one that you like best.

For example, John may be the name of the child turned to.

J-O-H-N spells John and you're not it!

My mother and your mother
Were hanging out the clothes,
My mother gave your mother
A punch on the nose.
What colour was the blood?

Child pointed to picks a colour.

R-E-D spells red and
Out you must go!

My mother and your mother
Were hanging out the clothes,
My mother gave your mother
A punch on the nose.
What colour was the blood?

Child pointed to picks a colour.

Y-E-L-L-O-W spells yellow and
Yellow you must have on you!

If no yellow clothing is found on the person being pointed to, he is out!

Mrs White had a fright,
In the middle of the night,
She saw a ghost eating toast,
Halfway up the lamppost.

When I was young and had no sense,
I bought a fiddle for eighteen pence,
And the only tune that I could play,
Was over the hill and far away!

One potato, two potato,
Three potato, four,
Five potato, six potato
Seven potato, more!

All the children form a circle and hold out their fists in front of them. The child calling the rhyme taps, or thumps, each of the outstretched fists to the rhythm of the words. Whoever is tapped on the last word "more" lowers one fist and the rhyme is again repeated until only one child is left with a fist in the air. This child goes to the centre of the circle and is "on it".

Amen means "so be it"
A half a loaf, a threepenny bit
Two men with four feet
Walking down O'Connell Street
Calling out, "Pig's feet
One and four a pound."

A pig went into a public house to get a
*   pint of porter.*
"Where's your money?"
"In my pocket."
"Where's your pocket?"
"I forgot it!"
"Please, walk straight out!"

Eena, meena,
Tippy, tena,
A, baa, booshalom,
X, Y, number nine,
Out goes you,
Out goes one,
Out goes two,
Out goes the little girl
All dressed in blue.
Birds in the garden,
Fishes in the sea,
If you want to pick one,
Please pick me!

9: Queenio, Queenio, Who's Got the Ball?

Ball Games

One, two, three, O'Leary,
Four, five, six, O'Leary,
Seven, eight, nine, O'Leary,
Ten, O'Leary, postman's knock.

Ball games can be traced back to the ancient Greeks. In Homer's *Odyssey* white armed maidens play ball. Today, games involving bouncing or throwing and catching balls are usually played by girls; boys generally prefer the more rough and tumble games of hurley burley, relievio or football. Many of the ball games we are familiar with developed their sophistication and complexity after the Industrial Revolution; the development of towns and cities throughout Ireland and Great Britain brought in its wake large tracts of "hard areas", such as footpaths and roads to bounce a ball on, and gable walls in terraced streets to throw the ball against.

Children have long been their own teachers in the streets and have not learned their games from studying books or in the classroom, but orally, from each other. To our ears, most of these ball game rhymes are nonsense, yet they have an inbuilt coded language and a rhythmical momentum all of their own. The games contain a complex interwoven structure of rhymes, rules and rhythms which must be strictly adhered to by the participants, who require good skill, dexterity and concentration. There are "trigger" words which demand immediate and specific actions to move the game along, and heaven help anybody who breaks these rules, particularly when several players are in competition! No matter where you travel in Ireland, the following ball games, except for the odd dialectic pronunciation, share the same common language and catch phrases, such as "burley", "rolley", "plainy" and "backey".

Ball Against the Wall

Ball against the wall games are generally played by individuals who can use one ball or several balls if he or she is skilful. In these games it is the actions which are critical to the success of the game and these actions are triggered by key words contained in the accompanying rhymes, which have a language all of their own. The following are definitions of the commonly used actions which accompany the games:

Plainy: The ball is simply thrown against the wall and caught on the rebound. There are no accompanying actions.

Clappy: As for Plainy, but clap hands when the ball is in flight.

Rolley: Roll arms over one another when the ball is in flight.

To Backey: Clap hands behind back when the ball is in flight.

Hippy: Place hands on hips when the ball is in flight.

Tippy: Touch the ground when the ball is in flight.

Jelly Bag: The two hands are held together at the wrists and the fingers are spread wide apart to form a "bag" when catching the ball.

Basket: Weave and lock fingers of both hands together, with the knuckles facing backwards towards you; the ball is caught in the locked palms or "basket".

Burl Around: Turn completely around when the ball is in flight.

Over: Throw the ball overarm against the wall.

Downey/Dropsie: Allow the ball to bounce off the ground once before being caught.

Dashy/Bouncie/Dizzie: Bounce the ball off the ground first, before hitting the wall and catching it on the rebound.

Right Leg/Left Leg:	Throw the ball under a raised right or left leg to hit the wall first. In Dublin the ball is bounced off the ground first, before hitting the wall.
Underleg/Archy:	The two legs are separated to form an arch, and the ball is thrown from behind, under the arch, hitting the wall first. In Dublin, the ball is bounced off the ground first, before hitting the wall.
Backy:	Stand sideways to the wall and bounce the ball behind the back against the ground, before hitting the wall.
Walla:	Cross one leg in front of the other when the ball is in flight.
Stampy:	Stamp both feet on the ground when the ball is in flight.
Pipey/Pipsie:	Throw the ball straight up and catch it.
Uppy/Upsie:	Aim the ball higher up the wall.
Canary:	Use a pushing action, with the palm of the hand facing away, to throw the ball against the wall.

Plainy Clappy

Plainy, clappy, rolley, to backey,
Hippy, tippy, a jelly bag and basket.

From its definition, it is clear that this is quite a complex game that requires a good memory, apart from the agility to play the game once through successfully; by this time players are "for steadies": all players must go through the game again, but this time with their feet together, and not move from the same spot during the play. Then it is time for "right foot", when players go through the game as before, only this time their right foot is raised off the ground. Then, players do it again with their left foot raised off the ground. The Dublin version ends with the feet going through the motions of a step-dance. Any mistakes made during the game mean that another child takes the player's place; she goes through the same ritual until she makes a mistake and another takes her turn. When it comes to the first player's turn again, he or she can start from where they made the mistake the last time, and can keep going as many times as it takes to complete the full game. Another version of the game follows.

Plainy, clappy, rolley-polley,
Ding, dong, dashy, touch the ground,
Burl around.

I've a Bike

I've a bike, a fairy bike,	Plainy
I only got it last Saturday night,	Plainy
I went up the hill,	Dashy
I went down the hill,	Downey
Under the arch,	Archy
And a rainbow.	A rainbow is described with two hands in mid-air while the ball is still in flight.

Sevens

The ball is thrown against the wall and caught as in plainy. If caught seven times the child can add another action to make the game more difficult. The idea is to see who is the most skilled player.

The following selection of rhymes can be performed very simply by beginning with plainy, but gradually adding more and more of the complicated actions. After adding rolley, backey, hippy and tippy, children can then use only one hand, first the right and then the left. Another way to play is to go through all the actions once and then double up and triple the actions; however, this is a tall order even for the most skilful player.

Ena Sharples went to bed,
With a hair-net on her head,
Is she alive or is she dead,
Or is she just a lazy head?

Please get off the grass, sir,
To let the ladies past, sir,
The ladies before the gents, sir,
So please get off the grass, sir.

Plainy marmalade,
Plainy marmalade,
One of the nurses,
Lost her purses,
Plainy marmalade.

Yella, yella,
What's for yella?
Yellow is the colour
Of the fairy's umbrella.

Mammy, Daddy, Uncle Joe,
Went to London in a po,
The po burst,
Daddy cursed,
And Mammy went to heaven first.

Mammy, Daddy, Uncle Dick,
Went to London on a stick,
The stick broke,
What a joke,
Mammy went to heaven first.

I heard the King say,
Quick march,
Under the arch,
Salute to your King,
Bow to your Queen,
Sit down, kneel down,
Touch the ground,
And a burley round.

Throw up the ball,
Let it fall,
Clappy-clappy,
Heely-toe,
Right hand,
Left hand,
Swale's mouth,
April, May,
Creadly,
Rooly, fiddle-y,
And burley round.

Charlie Chaplin went to France,	Plainy
To teach the ladies how to dance,	Plainy
And this is the way he taught them,	Plainy
Heel, toe, over you go,	Plainy touch heel,
	Plainy touch toe, Plainy
Heel, toe, over you go,	Plainy touch heel,
	Plainy touch toe, Plainy
Heel, toe, over you go,	Plainy touch heel,
	Plainy touch toe, Plainy
And that's the way he taught them.	Plainy

Are you coming, sir?
No, sir. Why, sir?
Because I've got the cold, sir.
Where did you get the cold, sir?
Up at the North Pole, sir.
What were you doing there, sir?
Catching polar bears, sir.
How many did you catch, sir?
One, sir, two, sir, three, sir.

Clipsy, clapsy,
Sidesy, backsy
Right hand, left hand
Both hands down
Wee burley, big burley
Dash.

Here is a game that two players can play continuously. One throws a ball against the wall and recites:

Matthew, Mark, Luke and John
Next door neighbour carry on.

One child runs in to catch the ball as it bounces off the wall, making sure to catch it before it falls to the ground. She continues to throw the ball against the wall and recites the rhyme, before she "carries on" to leave her partner to catch the ball.

Another game, which can use two balls, is based on the following rhyme:

Over the garden wall,
I let the baby fall,
My mammy came out,
And gave me a clout,
I asked her what she was talking about,
She gave another to match the other,
Over the garden wall.

Bouncing a Ball

Bouncing a ball up and down on the pavement soon becomes very boring, but by adding some rules, rhymes and difficult steps, the game is soon taken seriously. After bouncing a ball, a player is "for steadies": the rhyme is repeated while bouncing the ball, but the player has to keep his two feet together. If the player moves them, then he or she is "out". During the second time round, the player is "for right foot", which means that the rhyme is again repeated while bouncing the ball, but this time the player must raise his or her right foot in the air. If the player falls over or touches the ground with the right foot, then he or she is "out". After successfully completing "right foot", the player is now ready for "left foot", which is exactly the same as "right foot" except that the left foot is kept up in mid-air. The bouncing of the ball can continue as long as the players come up with new variations and skills to keep the game going. The following rhymes are examples of these games.

One, two, three, four,
Jinny at the cottage door,
Eating plums off a plate,
Five, six, seven, eight.

Mister Flynn
Broke his chin
Sliding on a banana skin.

Pounds, shillings and pence,
Mrs Bates fell over the fence,
She fell so high,
She tipped the sky,
Pounds, shillings and pence.

One, two, three, four, five, six, seven
All good children go to heaven.
When they die their sins are forgiven
One, two, three, four, five, six, seven.

Little Nellie in her tent,
She can't afford to pay her rent,
The landlord came and put her out,
Put her out, put her out, put her out.
It's not because she's dirty,
It's not because she's clean,
But because she has the whooping-cough,
And the measles in between.

Bounce ball, bounce ball,
One, two, three,
Underneath my right leg,
And round about my knee.
Bounce ball, bounce ball,
Bird or bee,
Flying from a rosebud,
Up into a tree.

Bounce ball, bounce ball,
Fast you go,
Underneath my left leg,
And round about my toe.
Bounce ball, bounce ball,
Butt-er-fly,
Flying from the rosebud,
Up into the sky.

O'Leary

There are numerous ball games which mention the name O'Leary and just exactly who this mythical character is nobody knows. At the mention of his name, a player's right leg is raised over the ball as it bounces. Here are several examples of these rhymes.

One, two, three, O'Leary,
Four, five, six, O'Leary,
Seven, eight, nine, O'Leary,
Ten, O'Leary, postman's knock.

One, two, three, O'Leary,
I spy Miss O'Leary,
Sitting on her bum, O'Leary,
Eating chocolate soldiers.

One, two, three, O'Leary,
I spied my Auntie Seary,
Going to the Lucan dairy,
Early in the morning.

One, two, three, O'Leary,
I saw Mrs O'Leary
Sitting on her bumba, O'Leary.

I love coffee, I love tea,
I love the boys and they love me,
Tell your mother to shut up her tongue,
That she had a boy herself, when she
    was young.
One, two, three, O'Leary,
Five, six, O'Leary,
On an O'Leary morning.

Long legged Italy,
Kicked poor Sicily,
Into the middle,
Of the Mediterranean Sea.
When Germany got Hungry,
She eat a bit of Turkey,
Dipped into Greece,
And served it on China.

One, two, three,
My mother caught a flea,
She put it in the teapot,
To make a cup of tea.
The flea jumped out,
My mother let a shout,
And in came my father,
With his shirt hanging out.

This is another "one ball game", during which the ball has to be kept bouncing continuously while the player throws his or her leg over the ball, repeats the rhyme and counts up to twelve.

Number one, eat your bun
Throw your leg over
Throw your leg over
Naughty boy will never get over
Throw your leg over
Throw your leg over.

Number two, touch your shoe
Throw your leg over
Throw your leg over
Naughty boy will never get over
Throw your leg over
Throw your leg over.

Number three, bend your knee
Throw your leg over
Throw your leg over
Naughty boy will never get over
Throw your leg over
Throw your leg over.

All these ball games depend upon a hard surface for bouncing a ball, but the following rhymes do not require a footpath or gable wall.

Donkey or Donkey Rounders

Several players can participate in this "throw-the-ball" game. Cunning and quick reflexes are required skills. One good trick is to look at one player while throwing the ball swiftly to someone else; an alternative is to pretend to throw the ball to someone while immediately passing it to another player.

The players form a circle and begin throwing the ball to each other. Usually the throwing becomes faster and more erratic. There is no particular order for who receives the ball; however, a strict pattern for throwing the ball can be agreed upon before the game starts. Whoever drops the ball is labelled "D"; if they drop it again they become "O" and so on until they have dropped it so many times the player spells the word "DONKEY"; they are then eliminated from the game. The person who drops the ball the least number of times is the winner.

Queenio

Any number of players can play this game. One person is chosen to be Queenio and stands holding the ball with her back to the other players, who are a short distance behind. Queenio throws the ball over her shoulder and the rest scramble to catch it. If one of them catches it before it hits the ground, the player becomes Queenio. Whoever gets it after it rolls or bounces on the ground hides it behind their back and all the players say in unison:

Queenio, Queenio, who's got the ball?
I haven't got it, I haven't got it all!

As they say this Queenio turns around; the players stick out their hands separately to show that none of them has the ball. Queenio has then to guess who is really hiding it behind their back. If Queenio guesses correctly then she remains in the role; if not, the player holding the ball becomes Queenio.

Queen Anne

The Belfast version of this game bears a remarkable resemblance to a version published in *Chamber's Popular Rhymes* in 1870, though its popularity predates this. A sedan-chair was a covered cab supported on two poles. It was carried by two people, but only one seated passenger could be transported at a time. The chairs were extensively used in towns and cities during the seventeenth and eighteenth centuries. This is a very early version of the ball game "Queenio, Queenio".

Lady Queen Anne sits on a sedan,
She is fair as a lily, she is white as a swan,
A pair of green gloves all over her hand,
She is the fairest lady in all the land.
Come taste my lily, come smell my rose,
Which of my babes do you choose?
I choose not one, but I choose them all,
So, please (Miss Nell), give up the ball.

The ball is ours, it is not yours,
We will go to the woods and gather flowers,
We will get pins to pin our clothes,
You will get nails to nail your toes.

The children take sides and form two lines. The Queen is chosen and stands or sits in one of the lines. The other line advances and retires and at the same time one of the players conceals a ball or small object in her hand. The players can place their hands behind their backs or fold their arms or put their hands under their armpits, confusing the Queen as to who has the ball. The other side has to guess which of the players on the opposite side has the ball. The line which has the ball starts the game by advancing and reciting the first six lines of the verse. Queen Anne answers the question by reciting lines seven and eight, and names one of the girls on the opposite side whom she suspects has the ball. The players in turn recite the last four lines. If Queen Anne is right in her guess, the lines change sides, but if she is wrong the line with the player who has the ball retires triumphantly and the player holds it up to show the Queen she was wrong. The girls all curtsey when leaving the Queen's presence. Another girl in the line takes the ball and the game continues until the holder of the ball is correctly named.

10: Skipping Time!

Skipping Games

Dublin on the Liffey,
Yorkshire on the ooze,
Belfast on the Lagan,
And McMordie on the booze.

In ancient Greece they used vine strands, in the hop season in England they used the hop stem stripped of its leaves, but in Belfast we had our own internationally famous ropeworks. No matter what century, no matter what country, one game in common during springtime was skipping.

The great thing about skipping is that it can be played by one or two children; at its best, however, and depending upon the length of the rope, up to a dozen players can be involved at once. Solo skipping does not have the variation or "crack" that several players can create when skipping together. However, one child can learn to run and skip along the street or use various routines to skip or jump over the rope on the spot. Each time the actions become faster and faster, until exhaustion sets in or the player trips on the rope and has to start all over again. If another player wants to join, the solo skipper chants:

I call in my sister

and then announces the Christian name of the "sister", who runs into the rope. The two commence to skip in unison:

Oh! (Molly)
My bonny, bonny, Molly
All the boys and all the girls
They love (Molly).

A further player can cram in behind and create further turmoil – the crack can be great! Another variation of this game, sometimes called "Visiting" is as follows. While the solo skipper is skipping, she calls in another, who jumps in to face her. The two continue to skip in unison for a while, until the "visitor" runs off again, leaving the solo skipper free to call another player!

Somebody under the bed,
Whoever can it be,
I feel so very nervous,
I call for (Mary) in.
(Mary) lights a candle,
Nobody there,
I die didily-i and
Out goes she.

As soon as there are at least three players, the variety of games that can be played is infinite. The simplest and best-known games are those that begin with "salt". Two players turn the rope at a moderate pace, while one child skips; they all recite the words in a strict tempo, but the more they repeat the rhyme, the faster the rope is turned until the skipper trips on it – it is now her turn to hold one end of the rope.

Salt, mustard, cayenne, pepper.

Salt, mustard, ginger, cayenne,
Vinegar, salt, pepper.

Moving on to the more complicated games, it is worth noting that amidst all the clamour of these incantations are specific instructions to the players, which must be acted upon. Some of these action phrases are "Pick it up, Out goes she, I walked out, G-O stands for GO, O-U-T spells OUT". The punishment for ignoring these commands is to hold the end of the rope. Of course, the player can always get revenge by giving the rope a quick pull while the next player is skipping. These skipping games also use the same techniques as the solo skipper for calling another player in or out.

Keep the kettle boiling
Or you won't get your tea
When it's ready
Call for (Jane).

Keep the kettle boiling
Miss the rope you're out
If you had a been
Where I had been
You wouldn't ha' been put out.

Early in the morning at half past eight,
The postman came knocking at the gate,
I spy a lark, shining in the dark,
Echo, echo, G-O GO!

Early in the morning at eight o' clock,
You shall hear the postman's knock,
Post boy, post boy, drop your letter,
Lady, lady, pick it up.

Player bends to touch the ground.

Dancing Dolly had no sense,
She bought a fiddle for eighteen pence,
But the only tune that she could play,
Was "Sally, get out of the donkey's way."

Datsey, datsey
Miss the rope
You are out.

House to let
Apply within
When you go out
Somebody else comes in!

Jelly on a plate
Jelly on a plate
Wibbly, wobbly, wibbly, wobbly,

(player wriggles while skipping)

Jelly on a plate.

Sausage on the pan
Sausage on the pan
Turn it over, turn it over

(player turns around while skipping)

Sausage on the pan.

Money on the floor
Money on the floor
Pick it up, pick it up

(player bends to touch the ground)

Money on the floor.

I know a lady
Her name is Miss
And all of a sudden
She goes like this.

Player does the splits.

I love coffee, I love tea,
I love the girls and the girls love me,
I wish my mother would hold her tongue,
For she had a boy when she was young.

I love coffee,
I love tea,
I love the boys,
And the boys love me.

These two rhymes use two skippers only.

Two little sausages,
Frying on the pan,
One got burnt,
And the other said scram.

Two little dicky birds sat on the wall,
One called Peter, the other called Paul.
Fly away, Peter. Fly away, Paul.
Come back, Peter. Come back, Paul.

Sometimes when several girls jump in to skip, they say: "All in for a bottle of gin"; when they rush out, they say: "All out, for a bottle of stout."

Teddy bears became very popular in 1907 after President "Teddy" Roosevelt returned empty handed from a bear hunting expedition. He was presented with one as a consolation prize. Whether this gave birth to a whole new series of skipping games featuring the teddy bear is a matter for conjecture, but the ones that follow are full of key action words.

Teddy Bear, Teddy Bear,
Go upstairs,
Teddy Bear, Teddy Bear,
Say your prayers.
Teddy Bear, Teddy Bear,
Put out the light,
Teddy Bear, Teddy Bear,
Say goodnight.

Players run away.

Teddy Bear, Teddy Bear,
Turn right around,
Teddy Bear, Teddy Bear,
Touch the ground.
Teddy Bear, Teddy Bear,
Show your shoe,
Teddy Bear, Teddy Bear,
Run right through.

On the Hillside

This is a similar action game to "Teddy Bear":

> I went down-town to see Mrs Brown,
> She gave me a nickel,
> So I bought a pickle,
> The pickle was sour, so I bought a flower,
> The flower wouldn't smell, so I bought a bell,
> The bell wouldn't ring, so I began to sing.
> On the hillside stands a lady,
> Who she is I do not know,
> All she wants is gold and silver,
> All she wants is a nice young man.
> Lady, lady, tip the ground,
> Lady, lady, turn around,
> Lady, lady, show your shoe,
> Lady, lady, run right through.

Counting

One of the important features of skipping games is their educational value by teaching children how to count or recite the months of the year or the letters of the alphabet.

> Cinderella, all dressed in yellow,
> Went upstairs to see her fellow,
> Made a mistake and kissed a snake,
> How many doctors did it take?
> One, two, three, four.

Count faster and faster.

> Cinderella, all dressed in yellow,
> Went downstairs to get some mustard,
> On her way her pyjamas bursted,
> How many people were disgusted?
> One, two, three, four.

Count faster and faster.

Charlie Chaplin

Charlie Chaplin sat on a pin
How many miles did it go in?
One, two, three, four.

Count faster and faster.

Mickey Mouse built a house
How many bricks did he use?
One, two, three, four.

Count faster and faster.

A very good morning to you, sir.
Where have you been, sir?
Been to the North Pole, sir.
What were you doing there, sir?
Catching polar bears, sir.
How many did you catch, sir?
One, two, three, four.

Count faster and faster.

Mother, mother, I feel sick,
Send for the doctor, quick, quick, quick.
Doctor, doctor, will I die?
Yes, my child and so will I.
How many carriages will I have?
Five, ten, fifteen, twenty.

Rope is turned faster and faster until the two skippers trip and they have to hold the ends of the rope.

An old skipping game called "Winding the Clock" was as follows. Two players turn the rope, while one skips and counts to twelve and turns around each time she skips or jumps.

The Alphabet

A-B-C-D-E-F-G-H-I-J-K-L-M-
N-O-P-Q-R-S-T-U-V-W-X-Y-Z
Sugar on your bread
Porridge in the morning
Cocoa going to bed.

A-B-C-D-E-F-G-H-I-J-K-L-M-
N-O-P-Q-R-S-T-U-V-W-X-Y-Z
Sugar on your bread
Take these salts
Or else you are dead.

Apple Jelly

As one child skips, the other players ask all the questions.

> *Apple jelly, blackcurrant jam,*
> *Tell me the name of your young man.*
> *A, B, C, D, E ...*
>
> *Strawberry, apple, blackberry tart,*
> *Tell me the name of your sweetheart.*
> *A, B, C, D, E ...*

As the alphabet is recited the rope is turned faster and faster; when the skipper is tripped at a letter, this is her sweetheart's first initial. The questions continue as to the sweetheart's occupation.

> *What will your sweetheart be?*
> *A tinker, a tailor*
> *A soldier, a sailor*
> *A rich man, a poor man*
> *A beggar-man, a thief*
> *A doctor, a lawyer*
> *A minister, a priest.*

The rope is turned faster and faster until the skipper is again tripped, hoping that she is not stopped at "poor man, beggar man or thief". The questions continue, covering the months of the year.

> *Will you marry him?*
> *Yes, no, certainly so.*
> *When will you marry him?*
> *January, February, March ...*

... until the skipper is stopped.

> *What will you wear?*
> *Silk, satin, muslin, rags.*

What will you wear on your feet?
Boots, shoes, slippers or clogs.

What will you go to church in?
A coach, a carriage or an ass and cart.

How many children will you have?
Five, ten, fifteen, twenty.

Up the Ladder

In this game, the skipper goes from one end of the rope to the other as if she is climbing a ladder; during the lines beginning with: "John came out" she remains in the centre of the rope.

Up the ladder, down the spout,
Into (Michael's) and (John's) house,
Peep through the window,
See who's there,
Ma, Da, sister, brother.
John came out to see about,
Who did he meet, but bandy legs,
Bandy legs turned in toes,
Turned up teapot, teapot, nose.

In an older version of the game, the girls ran in to skip, first on one foot and then on the other with a stepping motion. Here is a more complicated version.

Up a ladder, down a wall,
A halfpenny loaf will do us all,
A bit for you, a bit for me,
And a bit for all the family.

Two girls hold the rope and two skip in. One has to skip around the other without touching the rope.

Flowers

Two girls holding a rope secretly decide on the name of a flower. As the rest of the players skip, one by one, each guesses the name of the flower and then skips out, leaving another to skip in. Whoever guesses the name of the flower correctly has to turn the rope. The game can also be played using colours, fruit, countries and trees.

The Schoolmaster

Probably because of his authoritarian nature, the schoolmaster was always treated with disdain in skipping games; besides, children had their own way of learning – street games!

Our wee school is a nice wee school,
It's made with bricks and mortar,
And the only thing that's wrong with it
Is the baldy headed master.

(Teacher's name) is a very good man,
He tries to teach us all he can,
Reading, writing, arithmetic,
He never forgets to use his stick.

(Teacher's name) is a very good man,
He goes to Mass on Sunday,
And prays to God to give him strength
To bash the kids on Monday.

Dublin on the Liffey,
Yorkshire on the ooze,
Belfast on the Lagan,
And McMordie on the booze.

There are no prizes for guessing that McMordie was the teacher! Nevertheless, there were some good teachers.

Doctor Long is a very good man,
He tries to teach us all he can,
To read, to write, to spell as well,
January, February, March …

138

I'll Tell Me Ma

This children's skipping game has been adopted in Belfast by adults, who sing it with a passion more akin to a national anthem. Its literary style and lack of key action phrases set it apart from the general skipping games and illustrate how some street games like "The Grand Old Duke of York" or "The Wind" become absorbed into the repertoire of skipping rhymes. Belfast, of course, does not have the monopoly on this song, and other cities are just as proud of their versions – Dublin City, Golden City or London City. The Cork version has "spattering" instead of "blattering" and in all cases "marble eye" or "rolling eye" derives from the expression "roving eye": having an eye for the girls. The first four lines of the song became very well known at the end of the last century through the popularity of a music-hall song called "I'm Ninety-Five". However, the song is much older than that and both the words and melody originated from a Scottish "come out to play" song called "Weary, Weary", which had the first four lines of "I'll Tell Me Ma" grafted on to it.

> *Weary, weary, I'm waiting on you,*
> *I can wait no longer on you,*
> *Three times I've whistled on you,*
> *Lovey, are you coming out?*

> *I'll tell me Ma, when I go home,*
> *The boys won't leave the girls alone,*
> *They pulled my hair and they stole my comb,*
> *Well, that's alright till I go home.*
> *She is handsome, she is pretty,*
> *She is the belle of Belfast City,*
> *She is a-courting one, two, three,*
> *Please can you tell me, who is she?*

139

Albert Mooney says he loves her,
All the boys are fighting for her,
They rap at the door and they ring at the bell,
Saying, "Oh, my true love, are you well?"
Out she comes as white as snow,
Rings on her fingers, bells on her toes,
Aul' Jenny Murry says she'll die,
If she doesn't get the fellow with a roving eye.

Let the wind and the rain and the wind blow high,
The snow comes blattering from the sky,
She's as nice as apple pie,
She'll get her own lad bye and bye.
When she gets a lad of her own,
She won't tell her Ma, when she gets home,
Let them all come as they will,
It's Albert Mooney she loves still.

Repeat verse one.

The Wind

This game bears more than a passing resemblance to "I'll Tell Me Ma" and is not unique to Belfast.

The wind and the rain and the wind blows high,
The wind comes blattering from the sky,
(Ann Jane Murphy) says she'll die,
If she doesn't get the fellow with the rolling eye.
She is handsome, she is pretty
She is the flower of Belfast City,
She is a-courting, one, two, three,
Please, could you tell me, who is he?

(Albert Johnston) says he loves her,
All the boys are dying for her,
He raps at the window and he rings at the bell,
Saying, "My true lover are you well?"
Out she comes as white as snow,
With rings on her fingers and bells on each toe,
She says to Albert with a sigh,
"I'm in love with the fellow with the rolling eye!"

Or

The wind, the wind, the wind blew high,
The rain came scattering from the sky,
Down came (Nelly) dressed in silk,
A rose at her breast and a can of milk.
"Oh," said (Nelly), "do you want a drink of this?"
"No," said (Johnny), "I'd rather have a kiss!"

141

All the children sing the song, while Ann Jane Murphy skips. When Albert Johnston is called he runs up to the rope and continues to skip in unison with Ann Jane until another child is named. The game continues until all the players have been called to skip. When this is played as a ring game all the children form a circle and join hands. One girl stands in the middle of the circle. When she is asked: "Please, could you tell me, who is he?", she gives the name of a boy, who joins her in the centre of the circle. All the children continue to sing the rest of the song. The game continues until all the players have had their turn in the centre of the circle.

11: Pat-a-cake, Pat-a-cake!

Clapping Games

Patty cake, patty cake
Baker's man
Bake me a cake, as fast as you can
Mark it with a B
And put it in the oven for baby and me.

When two Americans meet, slap hands and say, "Hey, give me five, man!" they are, unwittingly, performing a very old and basic form of game known generally as "hand clapping" or "hot hands" as it is known in Dublin. These games have a very strict routine of clapping actions, which are carried out while two children are reciting or singing a rhythmical rhyme. Concentration, co-ordination and a good memory are required, as the various routines of the game are performed at an ever-increasing pace. Unlike street games, the accompanying rhymes to hand-clapping games are secondary to the game and are not literary in their content but functional jingles designed to keep the momentum of the game moving to a strict tempo. The objective of the game is to keep going as long as possible and to perform the actions quickly so as to complete all the routines without stopping or breaking the rhythm of the game. The instructions are as follows.

1. Two children stand facing each other.
2. Each child claps her own hands.
3. Each child claps a partner's hands:
   Right hand to partner's left;
   Left hand to partner's right.
4. Each child claps her own hands.
5. Each child claps a partner's hands:
   Right hand to partner's right;
   Left hand to partner's left.
6. Each child claps her own hands.
7. Each child claps the right hand of a partner with her own right hand.
8. Each child claps her own hands.
9. Each child claps the left hand of a partner with her own left hand.
10. Each child claps her own hands.
11. Each child claps a partner's hands as in step 5.
12. Repeat the whole sequence again and again, while saying the rhymes faster and faster.

In America hand-clapping games are referred to as "Patty-Cakes" and on this side of the Atlantic a rhyme entitled "Pat-a-Cake, Pat-a-Cake" was first collected in 1698.

Patty cake, patty cake
Baker's man
Bake me a cake, as fast as you can
Mark it with a B
And put it in the oven for baby and me.

At the end of the last century, children in the streets of Washington played a hand-clapping game to the accompaniment of "Pease, porridge hot"; at the beginning of this century, the same game was being played in Ireland.

Pease parritch hot,
Pease parritch cold,
Pease parritch in a pot,
Nine days old.
Some like it hot,
Some like it cold,
Some like it in a pot,
Nine days old.

My Mummy Told Me

My mummy told me,
If I was a goody,
That she would buy me,
A rubber dolly.
My auntie told her, I kissed a soldier,
Now she won't buy me a rubber dolly.

Mrs D, Mrs I, Mrs F, F, I
Mrs C, Mrs U, Mrs L, T, Y
D-I-F-F-I-C-U-L-T-Y
DIFFICULTY!

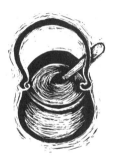

A Sailor Went to Sea, Sea, Sea

A sailor went to sea, sea, sea,
To see what he could see, see, see,
But all that he could see, see, see,
Was the bottom of the deep blue sea, sea, sea.

A sailor went to chop, chop, chop …

A sailor went to knee, knee, knee …

A sailor went to toe, toe, toe …

"A Sailor Went" has a more complicated structure than other clapping games, because players have to touch various parts of their bodies without breaking the rhythm of the game. At "chop, chop, chop" they enact a chopping action into the bend of their elbows. Once the basic clapping pattern has been established the children should be able to move on to a more complicated pattern.

1. Two children stand facing each other.
2. Each child claps her own hands.
3. Each child claps a partner's hands:
    Right hand to right hand and then,
    Left hand to left hand.
4. Each child claps her own hands.
5. Each child raises her right hand to shoulder level with the palm down and lowers her left hand to waist level with the palm up. Both children lower and raise hands at the same time to clap.
6. Each partner claps her own hands.

7. Each child raises her left hand to shoulder level with the palm down and lowers her right hand to waist level with the palm up. Both children lower and raise hands at the same time to clap.

8. Repeat the sequence and chant one of the following rhymes.

> *All the girls in France do the hula, hula dance,*
> *And the dance that they do is enough to kill a shrew,*
> *And the shrew that they kill is enough to take a pill,*
> *And the pill that they take is enough to fry a snake,*
> *And the snake that they fry is enough to tell a lie,*
> *And the lie that they tell is enough to go to hell,*
> *And the hell that they go to is enough to stand on your toes.*

At the word "toe" the children stand on their tip toes.

> *My mammy sent me to the shops one day*
> *And told me what to say, say, say*
> *And there I met a pretty little boy/girl*
> *Who offered me to stay, stay, stay.*
> *He/she offered me some peaches*
> *He/she offered me some pears*
> *He/she offered me his/her twenty cents*
> *To kiss him/her on the stairs, stairs, stairs.*
> *I do not want your peaches*
> *I do not want your pears*
> *I do not want your twenty cents*
> *To kiss you on the stairs.*

Three, Six, Nine

Three, six, nine
The goose drank wine
The monkey chewed tobacco
In the streets of Caroline (On the street car line).
The lion broke (The line broke)
And the monkey got choked
And they all went to heaven
In a little rowing boat.
Clap! Clap!

Under the Bramble Bushes

Under the bramble bushes
Under the sea, boom, boom, boom
True love for you, my darling
True love for me.
And we'll get married
And have a family
A girl for me
And a boy for you!

Under the bramble bushes
Under the sea, boom, boom, boom
Johnny broke a bottle
And he blamed it on me.
I told my Mama
I told my Papa
Johnny got hit with a bamboo stick
So close your mouth and say no more!

See, See My Playmate

See, see my playmate,
Come out and play with me,
And bring your dollies too,
Climb up the apple tree,
Slide down the rainbow,
Into the cellar door,
And we'll be jolly friends,
Forever more, more, more.
So, so, so sorry,
I cannot play with you,
My dolly's got the flu',
Chicken pox and measles too,
There is no rainbow,
There is no cellar door,
But we'll be jolly friends,
Forever more, more, more.

Have You Ever, Ever, Ever

Have you ever, ever, ever in your long-legged life
Seen a long-legged sailor with a long-legged wife?

No, I've never, never, never in my long-legged life
Seen a long-legged sailor with a long-legged wife.

Have you ever, ever, ever in your knock-kneed life
Seen a knock-kneed sailor with a knock-kneed wife?

No, I've never, never, never in my knock-kneed life
Seen a knock-kneed sailor with a knock-kneed wife.

Have you ever, ever, ever in your bow-legged life
Seen a bow-legged sailor with a bow-legged wife?

No, I've never, never, never in my bow-legged life
Seen a bow-legged sailor with a bow-legged wife.

Of all the children's street games, it is in the hand-clapping ones that modern life is best reflected, both in the topics chosen for the rhymes and in the use of contemporary vocabulary. There are clapping rhymes to popular songs such as "Hello Dolly" or to "Popeye, the Sailor Man" and rhymes about George Best. Rugby songs like "Dinah, Dinah, show us your leg!" are also sung. References exist in some British versions to "When Susie was a stripper or when she lost her bra" and "My Grandpa is a flasher"; obviously there is a greater emphasis on sexuality in lyrics, possibly indicating that children mature younger these days and lose their youthfulness at a much earlier age than did their ancestors who innocently sang: "Pease, porridge hot" and "Pat-a-cake".

Acknowledgements

I would like to thank the following people who have greatly assisted me in the preparation of this book:

Brendan Colgan, who has given me great moral support and encouragement. Without his help and guidance I could not have prepared such detailed information on Skipping, Clapping, Ball Games and Counting Rhymes. His extensive collection of children's games from the Lower Falls is unsurpassed and deserves wider recognition.

Eilis Brady, who has done marvellous work in her collection of Dublin street games. Thanks for permission to use material from "All in! All in!"

David Hammond, who gave me permission to use material from *Songs of Belfast.*

To Noel and Michael McHale and the "Mackintosh Finale" music programme: many, many thanks for taking the time and trouble to "input" and print the music for me.

To my wife, Jane, for moral support, encouragement and general guidance.

Lastly, to Appletree Press, who took an immediate interest in the project and have given me the opportunity to bring these games from the "Singing Street" to a much wider audience.

Maurice Leyden